AMAZING
PLANTS AND TREES
OF THE WORLD

Amreen Toor holds a Master's degree in Mass Communication from Panjab University along with a Diploma in Creative Writing from IGNOU. She worked as an assistant editor for the *Limca Book of Records* and then ventured into the field of curriculum and product development for Junior and Middle programmes for schools affiliated to both Central and state education boards. Working as part of a vendor team for Google, she started out in the vast and ever-expanding field of localization: writing and translating content in Hindi for various Google products.

Presently, she works as a freelance translator and transcreator, providing subtitles in both Hindi and English for movies and TV series for entertainment giants like Netflix, Amazon Prime and independent production houses. An ardent dog lover, she lives in Gurugram with her husband and two children.

501 FACTS FACTORY

AMAZING PLANTS AND TREES OF THE WORLD

Amreen Toor

hachette INDIA

First published in 2020 by Hachette India
(Registered name: Hachette Book Publishing India Pvt. Ltd)
An Hachette UK company
www.hachetteindia.com

SRD

ISBN 978-93-89253-27-6

Hachette Book Publishing India Pvt. Ltd
4th & 5th Floors, Corporate Centre
Plot No. 94, Sector 44, Gurugram - 122003, India

Typeset by Manmohan Kumar, Delhi

Printed and bound in India
by Manipal Technologies Limited, Manipal

MIX
Paper from responsible sources
FSC™ C043100

CONTENTS

1

TREES

Trees are our lifeline. Irrespective of their size, shape and colour, these woody-tissue organisms may be the greatest gift to humankind.

1 **A tree that's older than the Egyptian pyramids!** The oldest living tree in the world is called Methuselah. Belonging to the bristlecone pine tree species, it stands on the White Mountain in Inyo National Forest, California, USA. In the summer of 1957, American scientist Dr Edmund Schulman, along with his assistant, discovered sixteen bristlecone pine trees, all of which were believed to be over 4,000 years old. Upon checking for their exact age, Methuselah was found to be more than 4,800 years old. Of the trees discovered, nine of them are in the area popularly known as the 'Methuselah Walk'.

2 **The largest banyan tree in the world is in Kolkata, India.** Located in Acharya Jagadish Chandra Bose Botanical Garden, the Great Banyan is more than 250 years old. Its highest branch rises to 24.5 metres from the ground. Spread over 4.5 acres of land, it is also the widest tree in the world. It has about 3,772 aerial roots reaching down to the ground. Unfortunately, the tree's main trunk had to be cut off in 1925 because of an extended fungal attack, but despite removing 15.5 metres of trunk, the leftover tree has stayed

quite healthy. The tree is now protected by a 330-metre long track around it, even as the tree continues to grow beyond it.

3 **A wish-fulfilling tree.** The *bargad* or banyan tree, according to Hindu mythology, is known as Kalpavriksha, a tree that fulfils wishes and grants material gain. The tree lives long (some are known to be 200 years old!) and therefore signifies immortality, according to Hindu scriptures. Its leaves are used in various rituals and religious practices.

4 **Angel Oak is the oldest living oak tree in the world.** The southern live oak, also known as the live oak, is commonly found in the states of Georgia, Florida, Louisiana and Mississippi in the USA. Angel Oak is a southern live oak believed to be about 400 to 500 years old in Angel Oak Park on Johns Island near Charleston, South Carolina. It stands at 20 metres and measures 8.5 metres in circumference. The tree is approximately as high as a seven-story building. The shade produced by the tree covers an expanse of around 1,600 square metres.

5 **Sometimes, you can't blame a tree for being in the way.** In 1973, the world's 'most isolated' tree, Arbre du Ténéré (the Tree of Tenere) in the Nigerian Sahara desert was hit and destroyed by a driver who bumped into the tree while following a roadmap. Being the only tree over a distance of 400 kilometres, it had served as a landmark on the barren land!

6 **The smallest tree in the world is the size of your thumb.** The dwarf willow, or *Salix herbacea*, grows to only about 1–6 centimetres in height, with round, shiny green leaves that are around 1–2 centimetres long and broad. This tiny creeping willow needs moist soil to grow, and is found growing near waterfronts and streams. Found in alpine and arctic environments around the North Atlantic Ocean, the plant is resistant to cold and rain. The bark of this small plant contains 'salicin', which is a natural pain reliever.

7 **Trees have varying lifespans.** Contrary to popular belief, trees do not live forever. Some trees have a short lifespan, while others go on to live for hundreds of years. Some of the longest living trees survive best in extreme climatic situations. Coniferous trees like *chir*, pine and *deodar* are able to sustain themselves in very cold weather, and are found at the height of 1,500 to 2,500 metres above the mean sea level. Cactus, *babool, keekar* and *khair* are some examples of trees that live long in very hot weather conditions.

8 **Hug a tree!** To prevent the rampant felling of trees in the Himalayas, noted Indian conservationist Sunderlal

Bahuguna, along with Chandni Prasad Bhatt, started the Chipko Movement in the 1980s in present-day Uttarakhand, then a part of Uttar Pradesh, India. It was a people's protest against mindless deforestation. This was one of the first Indian movements that made common people aware of the importance of conserving forests. The word '*chipko*' means 'to stick'. The villagers would 'stick themselves' to a tree, hugging it tight, thus preventing it from being cut down by contractors. The Chipko Movement set the tone for other campaigns to protect forest lands and the wildlife in them.

9 **Planting more trees reduces soil erosion, which in turn leads to fewer landslides and floods.** Trees help in reducing the amount of soil run-off during storms and heavy rainfall. The roots of the trees dig deep and help in keeping soil intact, thus preventing erosion, which generally happens when the soil can no longer absorb any more water. In such a scenario, trees help against erosion by absorbing water from the soil, thus stopping it from washing soil away.

10 **Free, natural air purifiers.** Trees absorb carbon dioxide and produce oxygen, thus improving air quality. They also absorb harmful gasses like carbon monoxide from the environment. Certain plants help in keeping the air inside our homes clean and pure; these indoor plants release oxygen at night, thus cleansing the air. The most popular indoor plants that do this are the snake plant, the bamboo palm, gerbera, aloe vera and *tulsi*, to name a few.

11 **Trees are considered sacred in some cultures.** Many communities around the world worship trees as auspicious and harbingers of goodness. For instance, in

Persian and Zoroastrian myths, the Gaokerena was a giant haoma plant with healing powers; the juice of its fruit was said to give immortality to resurrected dead bodies. In India, many trees like the peepul and the banyan are worshipped.

12 **Pine trees are the most common species of trees.** Of the seven continents, six have pine trees growing on them. Antarctica is the only place on Earth where there are no pine trees and generally no vegetation due to severe climatic conditions. There are about 100 species of pine. They are considered evergreen trees and produce needles (adult leaves) that can grow up to nine inches long.

13 **Different parts of plants grow at different speeds, at different times of the year.** The leaves, the trunk and the root of trees grow at varying paces over a period of time. The leaves and the thick foliage are developed in spring, the trunk of a tree grows the most in summer and the root grows in the winter. As the cooler months approach, the trees go into slow mode and once the spring or warmer months come, the change in temperature and the variation in the length of day and night makes the buds on the tree active, which results in the birth of new leaves. The growth of the trunk is the most in summer because during this time of the year, the most rain is received and there is abundant sunlight, helping the trunk grow faster. The roots of the tree are most active in winter

as they search for moisture and nutrients, making them grow faster in the cold season.

14 **Trees work as natural air-conditioners.** An area with a high number of trees is cooler than a place with fewer trees. This is because when water evaporates from a tree's leaves, it lowers the temperature of the surrounding area.

15 **If you don't want trouble, touch wood.** The practice of touching wood or knocking on wood was believed to be a way to ward off evil spirits. In order to summon pure spirits, which were believed to reside in trees, people in olden times used to tap or knock on the tree for good luck.

16 **There have been many campaigns to save trees in India.** There have been numerous movements for tree conservation in different parts of the country. One such movement was called Save Silent Valley in 1978 in Kerala, India. It was aimed at protecting and conserving forests in Palghat district. Another movement aimed at protecting forest and wildlife was the Jungle Bachao Andolan, which started around early 1980s in the Indian state of Bihar, gradually spreading to present-day Jharkhand and Odisha. Such protests were also part of the Narmada Bachao Andolan, started in Gujarat by activist Medha Patkar in 1985.

17 **Save the rainforest!** Recently, the environment movement that has got everybody talking about it is for saving the Amazon rainforest. This forest has been burning since January 2019 and continues to do so. The fire could be spreading due to dry weather, but it was

believed to have been started by people in order to clear out pieces of land to build cattle ranches, for agriculture and so on. The Amazon rainforest is spread over 670 million hectares of land and deforestation has been a major threat to the forest. In 1993, the Rainforest Action Network was set up to protect them. Helping the indigenous population prosper, and reducing wood and paper consumption are some of the ways suggested to save one of the great natural wonders of the world.

18 **Trees get thirsty.** Just like humans, trees need water to grow. In a day, on an average, a tree consumes approximately 378 litres of groundwater. Water enters the root loaded with minerals from the soil and is carried up the tree's trunk all the way to the leaves.

19 **The 'Da Vinci rule' of trees.** Leonardo da Vinci was an Italian polymath of the Renaissance (fourteenth to seventeenth centuries) whose areas of interest included invention, drawing, painting, sculpting, architecture, science, music, mathematics, engineering, literature, anatomy, geology,

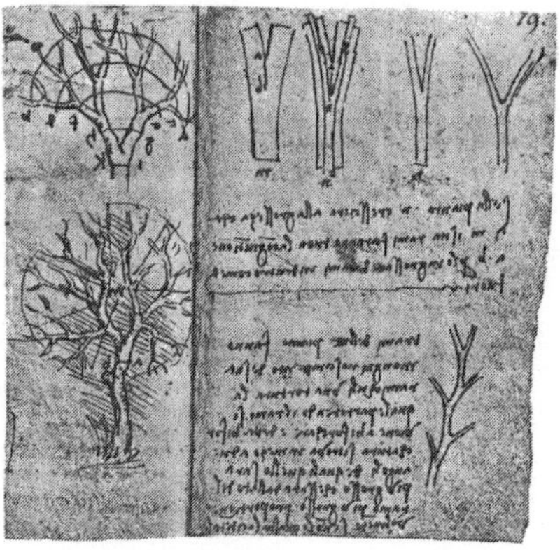

astronomy, botany, writing and history. He believed that if all the branches of a tree were put together, the thickness would be the same as the thickness of the tree trunk.

20 **Rainbow-coloured trees!** The island of Hawaii has eucalyptus trees of the species *Eucalyptus deglupta*, also known as the rainbow gum, the bark of which is naturally multihued. The bark of this tree sheds, revealing various streaks of different colours. Its bark is thinner in comparison to most other trees. When sunlight and air react with the bark, it changes from green to shades of red, purple and pink.

21 **Never stand under an oak tree in stormy weather.** Oaks have been known to get struck by lightning more than any other trees. The best explanation offered is this: Oaks tend to grow taller than most other trees and have a long lifespan of about 300 to 600 years. They also have a deep central root as well as hollow water-filled cells that run up and down the wood of the oak's trunk. These two qualities make oak trees better conductors and better grounders of lightning than trees with shallow roots and closed cells.

22 **A tree is mostly dead, but still alive.** An average tree comprises 99 percent dead cells, with only one percent live cells. The live cells consist of leaves, root tips and a thin

layer under the bark, called the cambium cell layer. It is this layer underneath the outer bark, which is the growing part of a tree trunk. It is responsible for producing new bark and new wood annually.

23 **Tree houses have fascinated people for a long time.** The earliest proof of a room up a tree goes back to ancient Rome when Emperor Caligula (who reigned during 37–41 CE) had a dining room made on a tree for a banquet. The Medici family that ruled between 1434 and 1737 in Florence, Italy, had gardens with a staircase leading to a platform on an oak tree. The Korowai people in Indonesia also lived in tree houses with their families. These days, you can find unique hotels and restaurants located in trees in both India and abroad.

24 **Trees as a birthday gift!** In China, as soon as a citizen hits the age of eleven, they are required by law to plant

at least three trees a year. The country has been following this practice since 1981.

25 **You can tell a tree's age by its rings.** You can also ascertain the age of many woody trees by reading the growth rings as seen on a cross-section of their trunks. The study of dating tree rings is called dendrochronology.

26 **Two types of trees don't have growth rings.** Trees produce growth rings because of the temperature changes that occur over a year, thus displaying when their growth slows down and speeds up. However, some tropical regions that have the same kind of climate through the year have trees that do not form very visible growth rings. Besides, 'endogenous' trees, such as the palm and banana, which grow by adding new material inwards, do not show growth rings.

27 **A tree helped to transform a young prince into an enlightened soul!** The Bodhi tree at the Mahabodhi Temple at Bodh Gaya, Bihar, India, is called the Sri Maha Bodhi. It is under this tree ((*Ficus religiosa* or the peepul) that the young Prince Siddhartha sat for meditation and became the Buddha ('the awakened one') upon attaining enlightenment after forty-nine days of meditation. The tree is associated with the path to enlightenment. The peepul tree is also known to release oxygen at night, making it one of the healthiest trees.

28 **Autumn colours may range from brown to pink!** The 'autumn leaf colour phenomenon' affects deciduous trees and shrubs, with the colour of the leaves changing from green to red, yellow, purple, black, orange, pink, dark pink, blue and brown. This change in colour generally takes place in the autumn months for a few weeks, hence the name!

29 **A sequoia is the largest tree in the world.** A giant sequoia (*Sequoiadendron giganteu*) tree named General Sherman that grows in the Giant Forest of Sequoia National Park in Tulare County in California, USA,

is the largest (volume-wise) tree in the world. It was named after the American Civil War general William Tecumseh Sherman in 1879 by American naturalist James Wolverton. He had served as a lieutenant under the general during the Civil War. The tree is about 84 metres tall with 52,000 cubic feet of wood. Giant sequoias grow tall because the tree lives for a very long time.

30 **Trees communicate!** It is believed that trees have feelings and warn other trees of possible dangers. American ecologist Suzanne Simard has discovered that trees send signals through the latticed fungi buried in soil. They also share nutrients through this network called the 'mycorrhizal' network. According to her, trees of the same species send each other carbon through soil, nutrients and other resources. This network also helps them to send out distress signals about dangers such as insect attacks, drought or disease.

31 **Trees also have family.** According to American ecologist Suzanne Simard, trees are more similar to human beings than we might know. Not only do they communicate, grow and age like human beings, they also recognize their kin. A mother tree recognizes and colonizes with her offspring and kin through the mycorrhizal network.

32 **Sometimes a single tree can make a whole forest.** In Fishlake National Forest in Utah, USA, there is a grove of quaking or Pando aspen trees, known as the 'Trembling Giant'. This amazing grove is a clonal colony of one male quaking aspen, which has been ascertained to be a single living organism with a huge underground root system. This Pando aspen clone is believed to be the largest organism

ever found and forms an 80,000-year-old forest with just a single tree in it! The tree weighs 600,000 kilos, also making it the world's heaviest known organism.

33 **Mark it!** A notch, mark or doodle made on the trunk of a tree will stay at the same distance or point from the ground even as the tree continues to grow.

34 **Brazil is named after a tree.** It is popularly believed that Brazil derives its name from the Brazil wood tree, which was discovered by early Portuguese explorers who called it '*pau-brasil*'. In Portuguese, *pau* means stick and *brasa* means ember (red stick); the tree shows deep red shades on the inside.

35 **The Amazon rainforest is the single largest oxygen-producing entity in the world.** More than 20 per cent of the world's oxygen supply is produced by this forest,

owing to the fact that it houses more than ten million of the world's species of plants. No wonder this forest is called the 'lungs of the planet'.

36 **The Australian eucalyptus is known to be the tallest tree in the world.** The last known measurement of the tallest specimen was 133 metres in height. Australia has about

700 species of eucalyptus, of which more than 90 per cent are found only on that continent. The bark of the eucalyptus tree dies and sheds almost every year, and a new layer is added to it. The most distinctive feature of this tree are its fruit, known as 'gumnuts'.

37 **The oldest living tree of the world is the ginkgo (*Ginkgo biloba*).** This tree, also known as maidenhair, dates back about 250 million years and was called a 'living fossil' by Charles Darwin, the English naturalist and founder of the theory of evolution. The name comes from the Chinese term *ginkyo*, which means 'silver apricot'.

38 **The first botanical garden was created in Rome.** Pope Nicholas III, a plant lover, founded the first certified botanical garden in the Vatican City in 1278 CE. The garden still exists in all its glory. It is spread over 57 acres of land, containing buildings and monuments from medieval times, along with beautiful flowerbeds, fountains, green lawns and an exquisite topiary (shrubs or trees clipped into ornamental shapes).

39 **The baobab tree is also a giant water vessel.** This tree is found mainly in Africa, although some species can be found in Madagascar and Australia too. It can store water and is a source of drinking water in the severely hot

months or during drought. When swollen, the tree's trunk can store from 1,000 to 120,000 litres of water. People cut open the tree's branches or the trunk to get the water and animals chew up the branches to quench their thirst. The oldest baobab tree, the Sunland Baobab on Sunland Farm, near Modjadjiskloof in Limpopo Province, South Africa, is approximately 6,000 years old.

40 **Approximately 170,000 pencils can be made from an average-sized tree.** The lead of the pencil is actually graphite. Initially, pencils were used to mark sheep, not to write with. Early on, the graphite sticks were wrapped in sheep skin or string for stability, unlike the wood-encased pencils we use today. Approximately 14 billion pencils are produced worldwide every year, which result in around 82,000 trees being cut.

41 **Carbon dioxide sponges.** A single 30-metre-tall, full-grown tree can absorb approximately 22.7 kilos of

carbon dioxide in a year, which is approximately the same amount of carbon dioxide likely to be produced by an average car being driven for about 41,500 kilometres!

42 **Baseball bats are made from the wood of the hickory tree while cricket bats are traditionally made from the wood of willow trees.**

43 **Of Brazil's many trees, the jabuticaba is a very unusual specimen.** Its fruit does not grow on its branches, but straight on its trunk! First the flowers appear around twice a year in a kind of white fuzzy growth. *Jabuti* is the word for tortoise in the local Tupi language, while *caba* means place. The tree was called 'tortoise place' most likely because the Brazilian giant tortoise enjoys eating its fruit that it can find close to the ground or fallen on it.

44 **Until recently, there had been no worldwide census of tree species.** In the year 2017, a huge scientific effort

was made in this regard and the results published in both the *Journal of Sustainable Forestry* and an online archive called Global Tree Search. It compiled and collated data from museums, botanical gardens and agricultural centres besides other sources. The findings showed that there are a total of 60,065 tree species currently known to science.

45 **There were no trees for the first 90 per cent of Earth's history.** The earth is 4.5 billion years old, and mosses and liverworts without deep roots may have appeared as recently as 470 million years ago. Vascular plants followed only about 420 million years ago, but even for millions of years after that, no plants grew more than a metre above the ground!

46 **When a tree needs to grow new leaves, it basically cuts the old leaf off!** A layer of cells starts to grow where the leaf meets the tree's branch and these cells finally separate the leaf from the tree, making it fall.

2

FLOWERING PLANTS

'A rose by any other name would smell as sweet,' wrote Shakespeare. The scientific definition of a flower may not be as poetic: it is a seed bearing part of a plant, consisting of reproductive organs, typically surrounded by brightly coloured petals and sepals.

47 **Flowers did not always exist on Earth; they first appeared 140 million years ago.** Before that, ferns and cone-bearing trees dominated the earth. Flowers are delicate structures and cannot be easily preserved. The earliest known preserved plant remains dates back to about 130 million years. It was only about 10 million years after that that the first flower bloomed. If all of Earth's history were compressed into an hour, flowering plants have existed for only the last 90 seconds!

48 **A flower shaped like a bird!** The Bird of Paradise is a beautiful, oddly shaped plant that resembles a colourful tropical bird. Native to South Africa, it is also known as the crane flower, because it also resembles a crane.

49 **The juice of bluebells was once used to make glue.** The sticky sap from the plant was also used to bind books, among other things.

The bulb of the bluebell flowers secretes starch, which was used to stiffen clothes and collars.

50 **The smallest flowering plant is the duckweed.** It measures 1.2 millimetres (less than 4/100th of an inch). There are about 38 species of the duckweed plant. The common duckweed, whose scientific name is *Lemna minor*, grows on the surface of water as a free-floating plant.

51 **What is 'baby's breath'?** The plant gypsophila is also called baby's breath because it was often gifted at baby showers in some countries. They are ornamental plants mostly found in Africa, Australia and Europe. It is considered as part of the family of Caryophyllaceae or carnations. It is used in soaps and shampoos because of its detergent-like quality!

52 **A country is known by its flowers.** Although native to Central Asia, tulips came to prominence once they were cultivated in the Netherlands (Holland). The word tulip is derived from a word *delband*, which means turban, via the French word *tulipe*. The Netherlands is still the main producer of commercially sold tulips in the world. It grows about three billion bulbs annually, which are mostly exported. Currently, there are around 75 wild species of tulips and 150 species in all, with over 3,000 varieties. The tulip is the national flower of Turkey and Hungary too.

53 Tulips can continue to grow as much as an inch per day after being cut.

54 **A special garden dominated by a single flower.** Although the tulip season starts from mid-March and continues till mid-May, the best time to visit Holland to see tulips in full bloom is mid-April. More than seven million flower bulbs bloom during spring at the Keukenhof Garden in Lisse, Holland, alone. Keukenhof, which means 'kitchen garden', is the largest garden in the world in terms of a single species of flowers – tulips. It is open only eight weeks a year and records about 800,000 visitors during that period.

55 **In seventeenth-century Holland, tulip bulbs were more valuable than gold!** The tulip symbolized immortality, life and love in the olden days, and in the 1630s, there was a kind of frenzy for tulips in Western Europe. During this 'Tulip Mania' the flowers became so expensive that they were treated as a form of currency. The lifespan of tulips is very short, being three to seven days.

56 **A plant that can be set fire to!** The gas plant, or the 'burning bush' as it is sometimes called, is native to warm, open woodlands in southern Europe, north Africa and much of Asia. It earned its name because its leathery green leaves, flowers and seed pods give off a strong lemon scented vapour which, on an airless warm night, can be lit with a match.

57 **The biggest flower garden in the world is in the middle of a desert!** The Dubai Miracle Garden is aptly named. Spread over 72,000 square metres, it has over 60 million flowers on display and 250 million plants. Located in the district of Dubailand, Dubai, United Arab Emirates, it was opened to the public on Valentine's Day in 2013 and now attracts up to 1.5 million visitors a year. The garden as a whole resembles the shape of a cricket stadium. The floral structures are changed every season from May to October so that repeat visitors get to see something different each time they visit. It boasts of a life-size replica of the Emirates Airbus A380. This flower arrangement found a place

in the *Guinness Book of World Records* as the 'Largest Floral Installation' in 2016. The varieties of flowers in the garden include petunias (the largest variety of flowers here), geraniums and marigolds. The garden is watered by reusing wastewater.

58 **Plants dislike human noise.** Noise pollution affects the growth pattern of plants. Some plants have a low threshold for noise and some can sustain themselves through it. Research has shown that plants can perceive light, scent, touch and wind, and are able to respond to sounds too.

59 **Does music help plants grow?** Experiments have shown that certain type of audio cues like vibrations stimulate the growth of the plants and help them flourish in their habitats.

60 **The dandelion is a completely edible plant.** The name 'dandelion' is derived from the French phrase *dent de lion* (meaning 'lion's tooth' and referring to the roughly toothed leaves). Dandelions might seem like weeds, but they are a good source of vitamins A and C, iron, calcium and potassium.

61 **Sunflowers move from east to west in response to the sun's movement.** Although a sunflower looks like one huge flower, it actually comprises a 'head' (the central black part of the flower) composed of hundreds of tiny flowers known as florets. It is these that ripen over time to become seeds. There are around 70 known species of the sunflower.

62 **The earliest fossil angiosperm or early flower is the *Archaefructus liaoningensis*.** It was discovered from layers of volcanic rocks from the Upper Jurassic period (around 145 to 163 million years ago), found between sedimentary rocks of northeast China. It resembles a water lily and first bloomed around 125 million years ago. It is believed to be extinct now.

63 **Some flowers bloom at night and close during the day.** These varieties are called 'night-blooming' flowers. Pollination is the main reason why flowers bloom in the first place. The shape, colour, size and scent of the flowers attract a particular pollinator. Certain pollinators come out only during night time. Some of the most popular and beautiful night-blooming flowers are the tuberose, moonflower and evening primrose, among others.

64 **The tuberose, also known as *rajnigandha* or *nishigandha* (*rajni/nisha* in Hindi means night), is a richly fragrant bulb.** It has tuberous and fleshy roots. The flower is used in the making of perfumes and garlands; it is even used in cooking in Indonesia.

65 **The scent of the night-blooming jasmine can spread to a distance of about six metres in the night!** The plant stays in bloom from spring to autumn.

66 **The largest non-branched inflorescence in the world is the *Amorphophallus titanium*, native to Sumatra, Indonesia.** An inflorescence is a cluster of flowers. Also

known as *Titan arum*, this inflorescence is known to reach a height of about 3.5 metres. The lifespan of the plant is around 45 to 50 years and it blooms only three to four times throughout its lifetime. The flower has a strong smell similar to that of rotting meat! There are folk stories that speak of elephants pollinating the titan arum, but we know that's not true!

67 **The plant *Rafflesia arnoldii* produces the largest individual flower in the world.** It is also known as the stinking corpse lily because the scent it emanates is similar to that of decaying meat. It is one of the three national floral symbols of Indonesia.

68 **The largest flower auction in the world is the one in Aalsmeer in the Netherlands.** Around 20 million flowers are sold daily at the Aalsmeer auction. This increases by around 15 per cent on special 'flower-gifting' days such as Valentine's Day and Mothers' Day. The flowers sold here are said to be subjected to around thirty quality checks so that they can be graded. The Aalsmeer auction is a Dutch auction, which works the other way round compared to normal auctions in this kind of auction – the price starts high and works its way down.

69 **Asia's largest flower market is held in Mullik/Jaganna Ghat in Kolkata, India.** This 13-year-old market has nearly 4,000 vendors selling blooms for weddings, festivals, temple rituals or just for everyday puja, from 3 a.m. Located under the Howrah Bridge, close to the River Hooghly, it sells flowers ranging from roses to sunflowers, marigolds to orchids, lilies to hibiscus, and more.

70 **The fine art of topiary!** Shaping shrubs and trees by clipping their leaves and branches into ornamental shapes is known as topiary. It is a combination of art and

nature, and through this a garden is turned into a beautiful landscape, giving it an extra dimension.

71 **Levens Hall, located in Cumbria, UK, is probably the oldest topiary garden.** It still houses original designs dating back to 1694 with 100 topiary pieces designed by Guillaume Beaumont (1650–1727), a French gardener of the seventeenth century. The design of the topiary includes geometric shapes that look like chess pieces! Other topiary art in the garden includes designs representing Moroccan pottery, peacocks, Queen Elizabeth and her maids of honour at her wedding, umbrellas and more.

72 **The Château de Marqueyssac, a seventeenth century château in Vézac, France, boasts of a beautiful garden.** The subsequent owner of the château, Julien de Clerval, in the 1860s, started to plant boxwood trees and had them carved

into various shapes. The present count of such trees stands at over 150,000. Over a period of time, he introduced walkways (running over five kilometres) and interesting rustic structures, adding to the beauty of the garden.

73 **Broccoli is actually a flower.** It is an edible green plant whose large flowering head and stalk is eaten as a vegetable. The word 'broccoli' is derived from the Italian word '*brocco*', meaning small nail or sprout.

74 **The lotus is India's national flower.** The lotus was chosen as a national symbol because of its presence in ancient scriptures and mythology. The *Bhagavad Gita* considers it a symbol for detachment because the lotus remains untouched by the muddy waters in which it grows, and like it, human beings too should rise above worldly attachments, the *Gita* says. The lotus symbolizes divinity, fertility, wealth, knowledge and enlightenment. The lotus is also a sacred flower for Buddhists, for whom it represents purity of body, mind and spirit. It is one of the eight auspicious signs of Buddhism – an eight-petalled lotus used in Buddhist mandalas symbolizes cosmic harmony, and the one with a thousand petals signifies spiritual enlightenment.

75 **International Flower Day is observed on 19 January.** The day is about spreading happiness by means of offering a simple flower! Also, 12 March is celebrated as 'Plant a Flower Day'.

76 **Not all plants need soil to grow!** Some flowering plants, such as orchids, do not need soil to grow. They get all their nutrients from the air. Many tropical orchids are

epiphytes. That means that they grow on other plants. However, that doesn't mean that they are parasites. Instead, their roots are covered in a membrane that draws water from the atmosphere.

77 **Some plants are sensitive to being touched!** *Mimosa punica*, for instance, will actually fold its leaves when it is touched, re-opening minutes later. It is a creeper or perennial herb often grown for its curiosity value.

78 **Cherry blossom ice cream is a real thing.** Known as 'sakura' in Japanese, the pale cherry blooms are a symbol of renewal and hope in Japan. The Japanese love cherry blossoms so much that they invented a cherry-blossom flavoured ice cream. Japan has been

celebrating the Sakura Festival since the third century. and it continues till date.

79 **The popularity of cherry blossom trees has skyrocketed of late.** Coca-Cola celebrates cherry blossom season with matching seasonal packaging in Japan, Häagen-Dazs releases cherry-blossom flavoured ice cream and Starbucks, the American coffeehouse chain, has a Sakura line of mugs and other products in pink.

80 **Picnicking beneath cherry blossom trees is a Japanese tradition.** *Hanami* in Japanese means 'flower viewing'. This often involves a picnic to enjoy looking at cherry blossoms as well as having food and drinks. Early Japanese texts mention that the tradition began with emperors and members of the imperial palace. Sakura trees continue to be a popular tourist attraction, and every year, the National Cherry Blossom Festival takes place when they bloom in early spring.

81 **There is an India International Cherry Blossom Festival!** Owing to the popularity of the cherry blossom festival in Japan, a mirror festival has started in India as well in Shillong, Meghalaya, India, usually in November. It is the world's only *autumn* cherry blossom festival. The festival is organized by Government of Meghalaya's Forest and Environment Department and the Institute of Bio-resources and Sustainable Development in collaboration with the Indian Council for Cultural Relations and the Embassy of Japan. Cherry blossom festivals are celebrated by around 28 countries across the world, such as Holland, the USA and South Korea.

82 **Bamboo flowers are rarely seen.** Some species of bamboo grow flowers only after 65 or 120 years. What is amazing is that all plants of one bamboo species develop flowers at the same time, no matter where they are in the world. They all also die at the same time!

83 **The agave, also known as the century plant, spends many years without growing any flowers.** It grows one single bloom and dies. This phenomenon is called being 'monocarpic'.

84 **Roses have a lot of uses.** The berry-like fruit of some species of rose are amongst the richest source of vitamin C. Roses are used to make jams and jellies, and are also brewed for tea. In ancient Egypt roses were considered sacred flowers and people used them during funerals to make a wreath for tombstones. The flower was also used to serve the goddess Isis in a sacred ritual.

85 **The Juliet rose is known as the '£3 million rose'.** This is because that's what it reportedly cost famed rose breeder David Austin of the UK to create the apricot-coloured rose hybrid over fifteen years. It was first displayed in 2006 at the Chelsea Flower Show, and took the floral world by storm not only for its beauty, but also because it was the most expensive rose ever developed.

86 **A plant that had no petals and lived underwater more than 125 million years ago is among the oldest known 'flowers', according to scientists.** The aquatic *Montsechia vidalii* was once abundant in freshwater lakes in what are now the mountainous regions of central and northern Spain. It looks like a weed. The fossil of this flowering plant was discovered more than a hundred years ago in limestone deposits, but scientists came to know of its significance only recently.

87 **The very expensive spice, saffron, comes from a type of crocus flower.** It is said that 0.45 kilograms of dried saffron requires 75,000 flowers!

88 **There are no flower species that are completely black in colour nor has anyone been able to develop any such flowers in a laboratory.**

89 **Poinsettias, a popular flower during Christmas because of its red and green colours, originated in Mexico.** In the language of the Aztecs of Mexico they were called called *Cuitlaxochitl* (meaning 'flower that grows in residues or soil') and now the Mexicans call it 'La Flor de la Nochebuena' (Flower of the Holy Night/Christmas Eve). So why are they called poinsettias, then? That's because, Joel Poinsett,

the first US minister to Mexico, brought them to the USA, in 1825.

90 **Sunflowers can clean up radioactive waste.** It seems that these flowers are capable of drawing out pollutants, including radioactive metal contaminants, via their roots. They then store them in their stems and leaves. Now you know why they are the international symbol for nuclear disarmament!

91 **The revival of a frozen plant – yes, it's possible!** The seeds of a 32,000-year-old extinct Arctic flowering plant, called the campion plant, were found in the burrows of squirrels, dating to the Ice Age. These were so well preserved by the permafrost in Siberia that scientists in Russia were able to bring the plant to life again in 2012!

92 ***Victoria amazonica* from the water lily family is an amazing plant.** Its round leaves or pads are so huge that they can be measure more than 2.5 metres across and they are so strong and buoyant that a small child can sit on them, and they would still float! It is said that a full-grown leaf can hold around 45 kilograms if the weight is distributed evenly.

93 **Nintendo Company Limited, a Japanese multinational consumer electronics and video game company based in Kyoto, Japan, developed a special flower to market their series 'Pikmin'.** This flower, *Bacopa cabana*, is also called the 'Pikmin flower'. Inspired by the yellow Pikmin, the Nintendo flower featured five white petals with a yellow centre.

94 **In Australia, there is an orchid (*Rhizanthella gardneri*) which grows fully underground.** So how did anyone find out about it? Even weirder! It appears that in 1928 a farmer noticed a sweet smell coming from the ground and uncovered the flower!

95 **Why did American inventor Thomas Alva Edison try to grow a 12-foot goldenrod plant?** This seemed crazy because this plant was considered a weed in the USA. It's because these plants are made of as much as 12 percent rubber. Edison's friend Henry Ford, founder of the Ford Motor Company, gifted him a Model T Ford car made with goldenrod tyres!

3

SHRUBS, CREEPERS AND CLIMBERS

Shrubs grow taller than herbs, and, unlike trees, they have multiple stems. They are bushy in appearance and have hard stems and flexible branches.

96 **Deciduous shrubs change with the seasons.** The life cycle of deciduous plants includes a growing season and a dormant season. Shrubs that shed their leaves with the onset of winter look the best in autumn when their foliage changes colour. Warm spring temperatures and rainfall wake deciduous shrubs from their slumber, and they begin to form new leaf buds. As the temperature continues to get warmer, the leaves develop more fully and reach maturity by the time summer arrives.

97 **Evergreen shrubs, as the name suggests, retain most of their foliage throughout the year.** However, even these shrubs lose some of their leaves in autumn, but not all of them shed leaves at the same time.

98 **There are two types of evergreen shrubs: narrow-leaved and broad-leaved.** The former has needle-like leaves and the latter has broad leaves.

99 **Chamaephytes are low-growing shrubs, in which the buds lie near the surface in order to minimize exposure to the wind.** Their seeds are also very close to the ground (or up to a height of 25 centimetres above ground at most).The importance of the bud staying close to the ground is so that they remain close to the soil surface layer. Staying low also protects it from bad weather and other dangers.

100 **Creepers grow on their 'bellies' around other plants!** They are weak-stemmed plants that grow close to the ground. Climbers, on the other hand, are weak-stemmed plants that cannot stand or grow erect without support. Hence, they climb on to nearby trees, structures or walls by extending their stems or branches.

101 **Climbing plants use different methods to climb.** Some vines use tendrils or specialized stems, suckers, thorns and other methods to support themselves while climbing buildings, walls or trees trunks. Climbing is a way by which the plant saves itself the trouble of making the stem strong in order to stand erect on its own. Climbing plants start by creeping on the ground until they reach a structure or another plant or a stem that then becomes their support to climb.

102 **Climbers are great space savers.** These plants can grow vertically, providing thick foliage without actually taking up a lot of space.

103 **The smell of freshly cut grass is a sign of distress.** Leafy plants release many organic compounds called green leaf volatiles (GLVs). When the plants are injured – when animals graze on them, or when we cut or mow them, or even when we handle them roughly – these emissions multiply.

104 **Vines can harm trees.** All kinds of evergreens and vines that grow rapidly are likely to harm a tree. They can wrap themselves around a tree, thus strangling its limbs or the trunk. Smaller vines, which are slow to grow, are less likely to damage a tree.

105 **What is the fastest-growing climbing plant?** *Parthenocissus quinquefolia*, also known as the Virginia creeper plant, is a deciduous climber and the fastest-growing one. It grows equally well in shaded areas, unlike other climbers.

106 **Do you know which is the fastest-growing evergreen climbing plant?** *Clematis armandii* (called Armand clematis or evergreen clematis) is an evergreen vine with long leaves and white scented flowers. It can grow up to 18 inches in a year on an average.

107 **What makes a climber climb?** Climbing is a behaviour that helps the plant survive without actually growing a strong trunk. The main reason why a climber climbs is to access sunlight, which helps in photosynthesis, by which a plant produces food for itself.

108 **Creepers produce new plants to cover a large area.** They grow horizontally and in doing so they produce new plants along the way in order to cover a larger area in the shortest possible time. Some creepers spread by stem growth, developing roots on the stem as they grow along the ground, while others send out runners that develop a new plant at the end.

109 **Creepers or vines can be invasive.** As the name suggests, invasive plants are those that spread across an area quickly and aggressively with very little or no help at all. They displace other plants and can also harm the structure or the area they grow in.

110 **Wisterias are beautiful, but they tend to become invasive.** The plant forms new roots at each node

wherever the plant comes into contact with the ground. The world's largest wisteria, in Sierra Madre, California, USA, is spread across about 1 acre and weighs 250 tonnes.

111 **Poison ivy is not only invasive but poisonous as well.** Belonging surprisingly to the cashew family, these vines grow in the shape of shrubs and contain a substance called 'urushiol', an oily liquid that causes irritant properties in various plants.

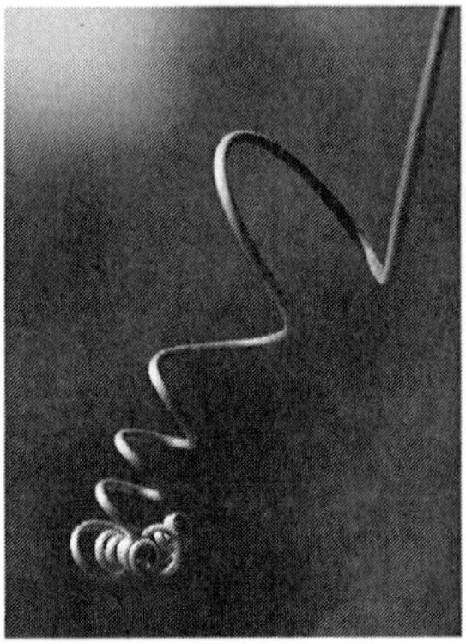

112 **There are two kinds of tendrils.** Stem tendrils are shoots that grow out of the stem. Leaf tendrils, although quite similar, are actually modified leaves emerging from the leaf node.

113 **Twiners are climbers that use their leaves as tendrils.** There are two types of twiners: leaf twiners and stem twiners. The first kind twist around slender wires, string, twigs or other leaves. The latter, on the other hand, curl around anything and everything they come in contact with. Some varieties of twiners become very heavy and large. Some of the common examples of twiners are jasmine, morning glory and wisteria.

114 **Scramblers are plants that have long, flexible stems that may look like vines, but they cannot climb on their own.** These stems have thorns that help them latch on to neighbouring plants or tree trunks. These plants need external help like being tied to a structure, like a trellis, to help them climb or stay up. Some examples of scramblers are bougainvillea and climbing roses.

115 **Some climbers have touch-sensitive adhesive pads that allow them to stick on to a surface.** These varieties attach themselves to the face of a structure or trellis and then climb up. If no vertical support is given to them, they can grow sideways, attaching themselves to anything in their path.

116 **An unusual group of climbing plants is the fern family Lygodium, commonly called 'climbing ferns'.** The stem does not climb, but rather the fronds (leaves) do. The fronds unroll from the tip, and theoretically never stop growing; they can form thickets as they unroll over other plants, rock faces and fences.

117 **Climbing plants start by creeping along the floor until they reach a stem.** Some tropical climbers start by growing away from the light, and once they touch something, the physical contact triggers chemical changes that trigger the climbing behaviour.

118 **A small shrub species is used in smelting iron!** *Phog* or *Calligonum polygonoides* is found in the Thar Desert in India. This plant is extremely hardy and its roots are used to prepare charcoal to melt iron.

119 **An unusually 'sweet' shrub comes from the savannahs of the South American country of Paraguay.** This is stevia, the leaves of which contain a substance similar to saccharin. It is more than 300 times sweeter than sugar. This plant is now used, especially by diabetics, as a substitute for sugar.

4

PALMS

The mention of palm trees transports one to a pristine beach, blue sky and water, children making sandcastles, people enjoying a game of volleyball and lounging on a deckchair with the sun shining on their faces. But there's more to palm trees than that!

120 **There are more than 2,600 species of palm.** Belonging to the Arecaceae family of plants, most of them are found in tropical, subtropical, and warm temperate climates. Palms are perennial plants.

121 **Not all palms trees are trees and not all plants called palms are truly palms!** Palms can grow as trees, shrubs and a woody vine. The sago palm, for instance, does not truly belong to the palm tree family. It is more closely related to pine trees than palm trees because it shows characteristics of a conifer tree: it bears a cone, which has a seed in it.

122 **Palm trees have two different types of leaves.** The leaves can be classified as 'palmate' and 'pinnate'. Palmate leaves grow in a bunch whereas pinnate leaves resemble a feather!

PALMATE PINNATE

123 **Not all palm trees bear fruit that are edible.** Fruit like coconuts and dates from certain varieties of palms are

delicious. On the other hand, the fruit of the sago palm is poisonous for both humans and animals!

124 **Palm trees have religious importance.** For instance, the day Jesus Christ was greeted by the people of Jerusalem, a week before his death and resurrection according to the Bible, is now celebrated as Palm Sunday. On this day, people carry palm fronds (branches of a palm tree) as a ritual. According to Christianity, Palm Sunday, celebrated on the Sunday before Easter Sunday, celebrates Christ's victorious entry into Jerusalem and marks the beginning of the Holy Week.

125 **Many products come from palm trees.** Coconuts, dates, betel nuts and acai fruit all come from palm trees. Oil is also produced from one variety of palm. The woody stem of the leaves is strong and is used as fuel or building material, while the leaves themselves can be recycled in the palm plantation as mulch, or can be used as a base for weaving baskets. Sometimes the whole leaf is used in fences and temporary constructions.

126 **The tallest palm tree can grow up to 197 feet!** The Quindio wax palm is the tallest-growing species

of palm trees in the world. The Mexican fan palm (*Washingtonia robusta*) can grow up to 98 feet tall.

127 **The fastest-growing palm tree is the Carpentaria palm.** This variety of palm can grow up to six feet in a year. Native to the rainforest of Northern Australia, the tree can reach up to a height of 30 to 40 feet.

128 **Palms like sandy soil.** Palm trees thrive in a moist and hot climate; hence most palm trees grow really well in tropical and subtropical climates. Sandy soil helps palms grow the best as the tree needs a lot of air pockets to spread its roots, a condition missing in clayey soil. However, they can be found in many different habitats. Some palm trees, like the windmill palm, can survive in freezing temperatures.

129 **Palm trunks aren't covered in bark!** A palm tree's trunk is the structure that holds the leafy vegetation above the

ground. It is sometimes fleshy and at other times quite woody. But it does not have the usual kind of bark. The 'bark' of the palm tree is not bark at all; it is made of 'sclerified' (or hardened) cells that are left over from the bases of fronds that have been shed earlier. The trunk's size also varies a lot, ranging from less than half an inch in diameter to up to 1.2 metres. The trunk's colour is usually brown, grey or green.

130 **Now, all about palm tree leaves!** Palm leaves are spear-shaped and have pointed tips with flaring pointed lobes at the base. The leaf's shape makes it look like a fork. They are longer and wider in the middle, shaped like a lance tip.

131 **The largest seeds belong to the coco de mer palm tree.** The seed is about 20 inches in diameter and can weigh as much as 30 kilograms.

132 **Palm leaves, like the bark, are also different.** The youngest leaves are at the top of the leaf crown. As the palm grows taller and older, more leaves are added to the top. Meanwhile, the older leaves grow larger until they hit their maximum size. When the leaves reach the base of the crown they are cut off from the vascular system, 'separating' their bases, which forms into new bark. Some palms don't drop their leaves cleanly, resulting in 'skirts' of dead leaves that dangle below the crown.

133 **Palm leaves symbolize victory and immortality in some cultures.** In ancient Mediterranean and Egyptian cultures, a palm branch was a symbol of victory, triumph, peace and eternity.

134 **South Carolina in the USA is also known as Palmetto State.** It is named after a variety of palm called Sabal palmetto.

135 **The shape of the palm leaf or 'frond' can help identify the species.** The most common shape of palm fronds is a feather shape, which is found on varieties like the coconut palm and the date palm. The second most common shape is the fan shaped frond in which all the leaves grow out from a single point. This category of palm trees includes the Bismarck palm, the Mexican fan palm and the windmill palm. The third category of fronds includes a cross between the feather and the fan frond, but in this shape the leaves grow from the extended structure and not from a single point, and this is called a costapalmate frond. The Sabal palm is a well-known example of this kind of palm. Another way of identifying the type of palm tree with the help of the fronds is to notice the direction in which the individual leaves are growing. Leaves making an upright-V are duplicate and the leaves forming an upside-down V are called reduplicate.

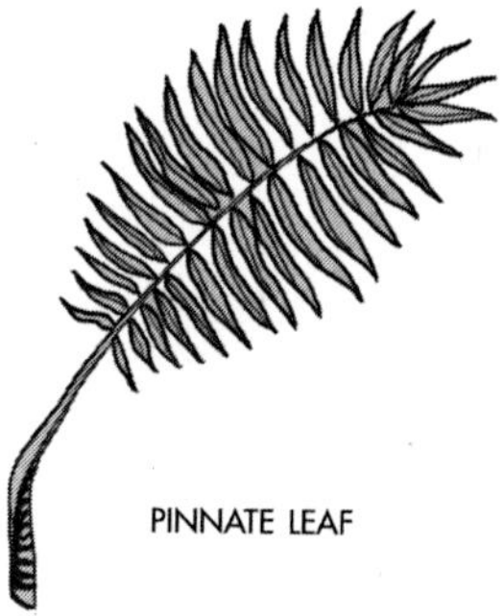

PINNATE LEAF

PALMATE LEAF

COSTAPALMATE LEAF

136 **The difference between a palm tree and a coconut tree!** The popular belief is that a palm tree and a coconut tree are the same. They are in fact two different species of the same tree. A coconut tree is a type of palm tree, but not all palm trees are coconut trees.

137 **The palm tree was once believed to be a symbol of life!** The Assyrians (in parts of present-day Iraq, Turkey, Iran and Syria in around 2500 BCE) believed that the ultimate symbol of eternal life was a tree growing beside a stream. The tree they valued most was the palm.

138 **Palm trees and humans go back to the earliest civilizations.** Archaeological evidence has shown that

the date palm was commonly used by Mesopotamian people for food and other purposes.

139 **Palms can live for a long, long time....even centuries!** This means that the palm tree you plant might outlive you. There is also recent evidence that at the cellular level, palms may indeed be the oldest living trees because their cells are not replaced with new cells, as is the case with other trees.

140 **Palm trees are preserved in some of the earliest flowering plant fossils that we have discovered.** Palm trees emerged 94 million years ago when dinosaurs walked the earth. Some species, such as *Nypa fruticans* and *Acrocomia aculeata*, have been identified in fossil pollen, marking the modern species as living fossils.

141 **Botanically speaking, palm trees are not considered trees!** They are grouped with grass, bamboo, lily, onion and orchids. There is an absence of secondary growth in

palm trees, which means that the length of the stem and root increases rather than the thickness of the plant. It is this characteristic that sets palm trees apart from other trees.

142 **Palm trees can be considered a type of grass.** It is scientifically proven that palm trees have more in common with grass than with trees. As you know by now, they do not have a bark making them same on the inside and the outside. They do not even create rings that determine the age of a tree!

5

FRUITS

Botany describes fruit as a seed-bearing structure in flowering plants. The 'fruit kingdom' also includes various plant parts not commonly known as 'fruit', such as bean pods, corn kernels, tomatoes and wheat grains.

143 **Strawberry is the only fruit in the world that has seeds on the outside.** On an average, a single strawberry has 200 seeds. The seeds that we see on the outside are the fruit's ovaries, called achenes (a small, dry, one-seeded fruit that does not open to release the seed). Each of these ovaries is a fruit in itself, with a seed inside it. Strawberries are actually not berries because a berry technically carries its seeds inside; instead they belong to the rose family. Despite having so many seeds on it, most strawberries are not actually grown from seeds! Besides being tasty, strawberries are also a rich source of nitrate, which helps in increasing the flow of oxygen in the body.

144 **Strawberries aren't technically berries, but bananas are!** Bananas develop from a flower with a single ovary

and have a soft skin, fleshy middle and small seeds. As such, they meet all botanical requirements of a berry and can be considered both a fruit and berry.

145 **You'd be surprised at the fruit that belong to the rose family!** Apples, peaches and raspberries are all members of the rose family.

146 **Not all oranges are orange!** In subtropical countries like Brazil, which is also the largest producer of oranges in the world, it is never too cold to break down the chlorophyll in the fruit's skin. This would mean that the fruit is still going to be yellow or green even when it is ripe. But due to customers demanding orange-coloured oranges, the fruit is treated with ethylene gas to eliminate chlorophyll, making the oranges orange.

147 Vegans, beware of figs! Figs are not always considered vegan. When pollinated by a fig wasp, the fig's inward facing flowers trap the wasp and the corpse is digested by enzymes in the fig.

148 **Only one orchid produces fruit.** Vanilla beans are the product of the world's only fruit-producing orchid, the *Vanilla planifolia*.

149 **Cranberries can bounce!** This is because the fruit has air pockets in it. This unusual property (because of which cranberries float too) was discovered in 1880 by John 'Peg Leg' Webb from New Jersey, USA, who experimented with cranberries and dropped a bunch of cranberries down the stairs. These days, growers still check the springiness of the berries to evaluate their quality.

They use a tool called the 'bounce board separator' to do this. The higher the bounce, the better the berry!

150 **Apples are better than coffee for waking people up in the morning.** This fruit is high in dietary fibre and pectin (found in the peel), which makes it a very good option to have first thing in the morning. The fruit's sugars also have an effect similar to that of caffeine. Vitamins from apples, specifically the skin, are released slowly throughout the body, making you feel awake.

151 **Some fruit are known as false fruit.** Some fruits are derived from the thalamus, or other floral parts of the plant, and not from the seed-bearing ovary. Some examples of false fruits are apples, strawberries, figs, pineapple and pears.

152 **The biggest naturally growing fruit in the world is jackfruit.** It is the largest tree-borne fruit, weighing up to 55 kilos. The fruit can grow up to 90 centimetres in length and 50 centimetres in diameter. Although a jackfruit tree takes about seven to nine years to bear the first harvest of fruit, this tropical fruit tree, once mature, can bear about 100 to 200 fruits in a year. Jackfruit is high in nutrition, packing in a whole lot of protein, potassium and vitamin B.

153 **Square watermelons?** Yes, Japanese farmers grow them for easier stacking and storing!

154 **In Belgium, there is a museum dedicated to strawberries.** The strawberry season holds a special place in the hearts of the people of Wepion, a small town in Belgium, so much so that a museum – the Musée de la Fraise de Wepion – has been dedicated to the fruit. During strawberry season, a small shop in the museum sells jams, candies, liqueur and strawberry beer. There are also guided tours of the 35-acre garden, which has local as well as exotic fruit.

155 **The Ozblu blueberry is the heaviest berry in the world.** Grown in Wilbinga in Western Australia, each berry weighs 12.39 grams.

156 **The thorns or spikes on the pineapple are the flower's wilted petals.** Even after the flower dies, it continues to stay attached to the fruit.

157 **Did you know?** Cucumbers are fruit.

158 **Bananas are a little radioactive in nature.** Due to the presence of radioactive isotope potassium-40, this yellow fruit emits a small amount of radiation. On an average, a single banana contains 45 milligrams of potassium, hence it emits around 3520 picocuries/kilogram of radiation. But it has been estimated that radioactive poisoning can affect you only if you are able to eat 10,000,000 bananas at once!

159 **The name of the colour orange came from the fruit.** The colour orange is named after orange, the fruit, but before that, it was called geoluread (yellow-red) in Old English.

160 **America is one of the biggest importers of bananas.** An average American consumes around 11 to 12 kilos of bananas a year. The Americans' obsession with the banana has been recorded in the movies with the Minions, who are especially fond of bananas. That's art imitating life!

161 **Bananas can be used as a ripening agent for other food items.** The fruit produces large quantity of ethylene gas, a hormone that helps fruits to ripen. Leaving unripe fruits like apples, oranges or peaches in a bowl with some bananas overnight would result in ripe fruit the next day!

162 **Banana cloning is a thing.** The bananas we eat today are different from the variety our parents and grandparents ate. Nowadays, nearly fifty per cent of bananas across the world are clones of a single plant variety called Cavendish.

163 **There are scientists who study fruits.** The study of fruits is called pomology.

164 **Eat a banana to feel happy!** Bananas contain a protein called tryptophan, which can induce a sense of happiness in people. This protein is converted into serotonin, a chemical that is known to make people feel relaxed, and improve their mood. The B6 vitamin present in bananas regulates blood glucose levels, which has a positive effect on people.

165 **The English word 'banana' could have originated from the Arabic word 'banan', which means finger or fingertip.** A bunch of bananas closely resemble fingers on a hand!

166 **Coffee is derived from the bean of the coffee fruit.** There are two main varieties of coffee beans – green and red. Red beans are less acidic and have a milder aroma, producing lighter coffee, whereas coffee derived from green beans is stronger in colour, smell and taste. The pit, purple or red in colour, is inside the fruit and is often referred to as a cherry.

167 **Coffee is second only to crude oil!** Coffee consumption across the world makes it the second largest traded

commodity; the first being crude oil. Surprised? Well, coffee is one of the most loved beverages in the world.

168 **The first ever Arabica coffee plant was discovered in Ethiopia by a goat herder.** He noticed that there was a change in his herd's behaviour after they had consumed coffee berries. The goats were more alert and energetic. He shared this observation with the locals and monks, who developed a drink from the berry only to realize that it helped them stay awake at night and pray.

169 **More than half the world's coffee comes from Ethiopia.** Arabica, which grows here, contributes 60 percent to the multi-million coffee industry worldwide. Ethiopia has around 15 million people employed in coffee production.

170 **The most expensive coffee in the world is Kopi Luwak.** It is derived from the beans excreted undigested by the Asian palm civet, and its unique taste is due to the digestive enzymes of the civet. This coffee comes from Indonesia and sells for over 27,500 rupees per kilo.

171 There are about 80,000 known species of edible plants on Earth.

172 **The world's smelliest fruit.** Known as the 'king of fruits', the durian is notorious for its strong smell. There are over thirty recognized species of durian, producing at least nine edible varieties. It was first discovered in Indonesia and its name has its origin in Bahasa, the language of Indonesia, in which it means 'sharp thorn'. The fruit's smell is so pungent

and overpowering that it has been banned on public transport in Singapore, Thailand, Japan and Hong Kong. Despite the strong smell, it is considered very healthy because it is rich in iron, vitamin C and potassium. It is said to improve muscle strength and skin texture, and lowers blood pressure. A small durian contains about 23 grams of fibre, fulfilling an individual's daily dietary fibre need.

173 **The Atlantic giant pumpkin is the largest and heaviest fruit (grown by humans) in the world.** On an average the fruit weighs around 68 kilos.

174 **Heard of the fruit salad tree?** This tree is specially grafted to bear several different but related fruits. There are four main types of fruit salad trees. The stone fruit tree has a combination of plums, apricots, peaches and nectarines. The citrus fruit salad tree produces lemons, grapefruit, oranges, mandarins and limes. The multi apple tree grows green, yellow, and red apples, and the multi nashi tree produces various kinds of pears.

175 **Coconut is a fruit, a nut and a seed.** It is considered a seed because it is the reproductive part of the tree. It can be called a fruit because of its fibrous nature. Since it has a single seed it can also be defined as a nut. Coconuts belong to the palm tree family.

176 **Fruit and vegetables don't die the moment they are harvested.** As you must have noticed, they continue to respond to their environment for days.

177 **Figs are the oldest cultivated fruit.** Remains of cultivated figs dating back to prehistoric times were found in a small village in present-day Jericho, a Palestinian city. It is believed that the cultivation of figs dates as far back as 11,400 years.

178 **One of the oldest fruit in the world is the African horned cucumber, also known as kiwano.** The fruit originated about 3,000 years ago in Africa. A fully ripe kiwano has an orange exterior with spikes and it resembles a kiwi on the inside.

179 **The largest producer of mangoes in the world is India.** The annual mango produce is about 16,337,400 tonnes a year, on an average. It is also the largest exporter of mangoes. Alphonso is considered the best variety of mango although this is debated by ardent mango lovers who have their personal favourites. Alphonso is also the most expensive variety of mango and is grown mainly in western India.

180 **Mangoes are the most popular fruit in the world.** Fresh mangoes are consumed more than any other fruit in the world. Mangoes originated in India, with the first tree recorded to have been grown around 5,000 years ago. Mangoes also come in orange, red and green colours and the colours affect the fruit's nutritional value and taste.

181 **The oldest mango tree is said to be in East Khandesh, Central India.** It is around 300 years old and still bears fruit.

182 **Parthenocarpyis is the process of developing fruits without fertilization.** Pineapple, banana, cucumber, grape, orange and grapefruit are some examples of fruits derived from parthenocarpy. These fruits, referred to as cultivars, are produced by keeping selective characteristics while propagating the fruit.

183 **The human genetic pool is stupendous.** Humans share 50 per cent of their DNA with bananas!

184 **In the American colonies in the 1700s, pineapples were imported from the Caribbean islands to America.** They were very expensive – one pineapple could cost as much as $8,000 (in today's dollars). The rich, when they had dinner parties, would display a pineapple as the centrepiece of the table! Pineapples were used not for eating but mainly for decoration, and they were eaten only when they would start going rotten. Some people would even rent a pineapple and carry it around a party to show off their wealth!

185 **Avocados contain more fat than any other fruit or vegetable on earth.** Also, their trees secrete an enzyme

that prevents the fruit from ever ripening on the tree. So avocado farmers use the trees as a storehouse for the fruit for up to seven months after they are fully ripe.

186 *Pollia condensata* or marble berry is the world's shiniest living thing.

187 **If you like strawberry flavoured food, here's an amazing fact for you!** The artificial 'strawberry' flavour takes more than 50 different chemicals to make.

188 **The name coconut comes from 16th century Portuguese sailors.** It is believed that the three holes on the coconut resembled a face, so the fruit was called by the word 'coco,' meaning 'grin' or 'grinning face'. The nut part was added later on in the English language.

189 **Canned pineapple was first made in 1901, but wasn't widely available until ten years later.** That was when in 1911 Henry Ginaca, an American engineer, invented a machine that could remove the outer shell, inner core and both ends of a hundred pineapples in less than a minute! He did this at the behest of James Dole, a big pineapple businessman in Hawaii, USA. This machine, known as the 'Ginaca machine' is still used in pineapple canneries today.

190 **Contrary to popular belief, there is no mention of an apple as the forbidden fruit in the Bible.** What is mentioned is the 'fruit from the Tree of Knowledge' with no further details about what kind of fruit that was. It was Hugo van der Goes, a famous Flemish painter of the fifteenth century, who first implicated the apple as the forbidden fruit in

his 1470 CE painting, *The Fall of Man*. After that, it became a popular habit to depict the apple as the forbidden fruit.

191 **In Roman times, people thought that the peach originated in Persia.** In fact, its scientific Latin name also reflects this: *Prunus persica*. Peaches were often called 'Persian apples'.

192 **The blueberry is one of the few foods that is truly naturally blue in colour.** The pigment, called anthocyanin, which gives blueberries their distinctive colour is the same compound that gives the blueberry's amazing health benefits. Blueberries were called 'star fruits' by North American indigenous peoples because of the five-pointed star shape formed at the flower end of the berry.

193 **The heaviest pomegranate weighed 2.60 kilograms.** It was grown by Zhang Yuanpeng in Liangshan, Sichuan, China, and recorded in 2017 by *The Guinness Book of World Records*.

6

VEGETABLES

Vegetables are categorized on the basis of the part of the plant that is eaten – for example, leaves (lettuce), stem (celery), roots (carrot), tubers (potato), bulbs (onion) and flowers (broccoli).

194 **The tomato is both a fruit and a vegetable.** A tomato is actually a fruit of the tomato plant although it is used commonly as a vegetable. There are about 7,500 varieties of tomato around the world. China is the largest tomato producer of the world, with USA and India as the second and the third largest producers respectively.

195 **Smart cultivation!** In olden times, Native Americans planted corn, beans and squash together, as corn provided a structure for the beans to climb, beans gave nitrogen to the soil that the squash plants utilized and the squash spread across the ground, preventing weeds.

196 **The heaviest tomato in the world?** According to *The Guinness World Records*, Dan MacCoy of Ely,

USA, holds the record for growing the heaviest tomato, weighing 3.8 kilograms, since 2014.

197 **Potatoes were the first food to be grown in space!** In 1996, potato plants were taken into space on the shuttle Columbia.

198 **Where is the single most fruitful tomato plant?** The tomato plant at the Epcot Science Project at the Walt Disney World Company, Florida, USA, is the plant that has produced the most tomatoes in the world. It bore 32,194 tomatoes and weighed 522.464 kilograms between May 2005 and April 2006.

199 **Fun fight with tomatoes.** La Tomatina is a festival similar to the festival of Holi. This festival involves ripe tomatoes instead of colours. The biggest tomato fight takes place in the small Spanish town of Bunol. Around 4,000 people gather every year and use about 1,50,000 tomatoes.The festival was made a household name in India when the Hindi movie, *Zindagi Na Milegi Dobara,* had a song in which three friends were shown participating in this festival.

200 **SOS by plants!** When some plants are attacked by caterpillars, they send chemical signals to parasitic wasps. These wasps swarm the plant and attack the caterpillars. Scientists call these insects or wasps the bodyguards of the plants.

201 **Did you know?** Surprisingly, eight-five percent of all plant species on Earth are found in the ocean.

202 **Potatoes are the world's fourth largest food crop after maize, rice and wheat.** Peru holds the honour of cultivating potatoes for the first time about 7,000 years ago. The potato has become so popular now that no cuisine in the world could survive without it. Potatoes are known to be rich in carbohydrates and they also have moderate amounts of vitamins, minerals and healthy fibre.

203 **Sweet potato is not only sweeter but also healthier.** Regular potatoes are low in sugar and fat when compared to sweet potatoes, but the latter is low in carbohydrates and high in vitamins C and B. It is also a good option as a pre-workout food because it keeps a person feeling 'full' for a long time.

204 Cabbage, kale, cauliflower, Brussels sprouts, broccoli, Chinese cabbage and savoy are all the same species of plant. However, they are so selectively bred that they no longer resemble one another.

205 **The city of Chicago in the USA is named after garlic.** The Native American word for garlic was 'chicagaoua'.

206 **What makes onions so pungent and tear-inducing?** An enzyme in onions comes in contact with oxygen and produces sulfenic acid, further breaking down into thiosulfinate. It is this process that generates its pungent odour. Thiosulfinate is also responsible for irritating the tear glands, resulting in tears. White, yellow and

red onions have a higher concentration of the onion enzyme, making them more effective in tearing us up whereas sweet onions, green onions and scallions have a low enzyme content, which makes them less pungent.

207 **Raw apples, potatoes and onions, all taste the same.** One cannot make out the difference if one eats them with a blocked nose!

208 **Eating lots of onions will make you sleepy.** Onions are rich in L-tryptophan, which is a natural sedative. They can also be helpful in treating insomnia.

209 **Halloween veggies!** Before pumpkins took over the festival of tricks and treats, turnips were used to make lanterns. They were hollowed out and used for lighting.

210 **Peas are among the oldest vegetables in the world.** They were considered very important by Egyptians, Greeks and Romans. It is believed that they originated in the Middle East, although the oldest pea remains were found in Thailand, and they were about 3,000 years old. The UK is one of the largest consumers of peas and it is estimated that, on an average, a person in the UK consumes about 9,000 peas in a year. Pea leaves

are considered a delicacy in China. Clarence Birdseye, an American inventor, entrepreneur and naturalist, experimented with the concept of freezing peas for the first time in the 1920s.

211 **Brinjal originated in India.** It belongs to the nightshade family of vegetables, which means that the fruit along with the flower can be eaten. The white variety is popularly known as eggplant in Europe because of its similarity to a goose egg.

In the UK, it is called aubergine. According to botany, it is considered a type of berry. If eaten raw, it might taste bitter, but it gets an interesting flavour after being cooked.

212 **Carrots were originally purple in colour!** The Dutch were the first largescale carrot farmers and at that time carrots were cultivated in hues of white, yellow and purple. Over a period of time, different strains of carrot were developed with a higher content of beta carotene, which resulted in the orange carrot. Eating too many carrots in one go can result in skin showing pigments of yellow. This discoloration is more visible on the palms and soles of the feet.

213 **Orange carrots did not exist until the Dutch crossed yellow and red carrots as an experiment.** They did this in the sixteenth

century for the 'House of Orange', the Dutch royal family of that time.

214 **Garlic was believed to ward off evil spirits and keep vampires away.** Bram Stoker's popular novel *Dracula* mentions the importance of garlic a number of times in fighting off the vampires.

215 **Many people think of the potato as a vegetable, but it's not one!** It grows underground like carrots, parsnips and other root crops, but the potato is actually a type of 'modified stem' known as a tuber.

216 **The most common colours of bell peppers are green, yellow, orange and red.** Red bell peppers are simply ripened green peppers, although the Permagreen variety of red bell pepper stays green in colour even when fully ripe. All varieties of bell peppers start off green.

217 Radishes were paid as wages in ancient Egypt to labourers who built the pyramids.

218 **Okinawan purple sweet potatoes, also called Japanese sweet potatoes, have purple-coloured flesh.** They tend to be drier and denser than the common variety of sweet potatoes.

219 **What kind of vegetables are 'fiddleheads'?.** This vegetable is actually the fronds of a young fern and many different species of fern can be used in cooking. They are cooked when they are still rolled up.

220 **It looks like red cabbage, but dulse is a type of seaweed that attaches itself to rocks.** It has become popular as it contains good amounts of iron, potassium and omega fatty acids.

221 **The hotness of a pepper can be measured!** The Scoville scale is used to measure hotness or to find out the spice level of a chilli pepper or anything derived from chilli peppers. The scale actually measures the concentration of the chemical compound called capsaicin, which is the most active component in pepper and responsible for the heat sensation. The higher the capsaicin content in a pepper, the hotter it is. The unit for representing the hotness value of a pepper is SHU.

222 **The hottest pepper in the world is the Carolina Reaper.** This small pepper, with a 'stringer' tail, is a cross between the Ghost Pepper (*bhut jolokia*) and the Red Habanero. The SHU value of the Carolina Reaper, as measured in 2018, is 2,200,000.

223 **Why are bell peppers not hot?** Bell peppers have no capsaicin in them, hence their SHU value is zero.

224 **The Romanesco broccoli, sometimes simply called Romanesco, is part of the cauliflower family.** It tastes somewhat like cauliflower. The most unusual part of this vegetable is its fractal-like look, which is definitely unusual and astounding.

225 **Despite the name, tiger nuts aren't actually nuts at all.** Instead, they are a type of tuber, though they do have a nutty flavour. They are high in fibre.

226 **Cool as a cucumber!** The cucumber, a natural coolant, is commonly used to soothe sensitive or sunburnt skin. The temperature inside a cucumber is 20 degree Celsius lesser than the temperature outside.

227 **Cucumber skin can be used as an eraser.** Next time you make a mistake while writing, instead of reaching for an eraser, you can rub the outside of a cucumber on the mistake, even written in pen, and erase it.

228 **The heaviest cucumber in the world.** David Thomas from the UK grew the heaviest cucumber, weighing

12.9 kilograms. The cucumber was displayed at the annual Malvern Autumn Show in Worcestershire, UK, in 2015.

229 **Cucumber can actually cure bad breath.** Fibrous vegetables like cucumbers increase the mouth's saliva production, which washes away odour-causing bacteria. In fact, holding a slice of cucumber between your tongue and the roof of your mouth for about 90 seconds helps limit odour.

230 **A top tip using a cucumber!** Before taking a shower, rub a cucumber slice on the mirror and it won't fog up.

231 **Also known as celery root, the vegetable called celeriac is mentioned in a poem!** In Greece, it has been used since ancient times and is mentioned in Homer's ***Odyssey*** as 'selinon'.

232 **Mushrooms, though belonging to the biological kingdom fungi, are also commonly considered vegetables.** The rare European white truffle is the world's most expensive vegetable, and its price can be more than 2,200 euros (approximately 1,73,000 rupees) per 0.45 kilograms.

233 **The nopal is a type of cactus, which is eaten as a vegetable.** The name mainly refers to cacti from the genus Opuntia, although this includes a large number of different species. Nopal is common in Mexican food in stews, soups and salads, and it is also eaten raw after removing the spines.

234 **Broccoli belongs to the cabbage family.** Its stalk and large flower like head is eaten as a vegetable. The word broccoli comes from the Italian plural of broccolo, which means 'the flowering crest of a cabbage'.

7

CACTI

A cactus is a succulent plant with a thick, fleshy stem that typically bears spines, lacks leaves and has brilliantly coloured flowers. Cacti are native to arid regions across the world and are popularly cultivated as potted plants.

235 **The word 'cactus' is derived from a Greek word *kaktos*, meaning a spiny plant.** Its plural is cacti.

236 Overwatering can kill cactus. Unlike other plants, a cactus may be killed by overwatering. It is a succulent plant, which means it can store water in its stem. Therefore, too much water can lead to the rotting of the plant, depending on the weather conditions and the variety of cactus. Watering also depends on the stage of the plant's growth.

237 **Cactus belongs to the Cactaceae family.** This botanical family comprises many species of flowering plants with succulent water-storing stems. The presence of a structure called the 'areole' sets cacti apart from all other plants in the family. Areoles (which are small, round, cushion-like mounds of flesh) give rise to flowers, new branches and spines.

238 **The oldest cactus in the world belongs to the saguaro family.** Known as the Old Granddaddy, this cactus was about 300 years old when it started to die around the 1990s. Not only was Old Granddaddy ancient, it was huge, about 40 feet in height with 52 arms (branches).This particular species of cactus usually grow arms as it ages, but not always, and a saguaro cactus without a branch is called a spear. It can take about ten years for a saguaro cactus to reach the height of one foot. At approximately 70 years of age, it can be about 6.5 feet tall and finally starts to produce flowers. At around 95 to 100 years of age, the plant grows to 15-16 feet, and starts producing arms. The Old Granddaddy at Saguaro National Park, Arizona, USA, got afflicted with bacterial necrosis, which typically affects older cacti. Before the Old Granddaddy died, it was one of the most visited and photographed cacti at the park.

239 **Saguaro cacti are naturally designed to survive in deserts.** Found mainly in the Sonoran Desert in Arizona, USA, every aspect of the plant helps it face harsh desert conditions. Its skin is covered with a thick wax-like coating that gives it a waterproof quality, and ensures that not too much water is lost through transpiration. The skin of the cactus is covered

with hard spines; its flexible bristles safeguard the water stored inside. When there is enough rain and the cactus is fully hydrated it can weigh anywhere between 1,500 to 2,200 kilograms.

240 **The tallest armless saguaro measured 78 feet (23.8 metres) in height near Cave Creek, Arizona, USA.** Due to the height of the plant, it was unable to withstand a windstorm in 1986 and toppled over.

241 **The largest known living saguaro, the Champion Saguaro, is in Maricopa County, Arizona, USA.** It measures 45.3 feet (13.8 metres) in height with a girth of 10 feet (3.1 metres).

242 **Cactus fruit is edible.** The fruit of many cactus plants is eaten by peeling off the fruit's outer layer. They are commonly used in making jellies and pickles.

243 **Cacti can store water in its stem.** Cacti thrive in a hot, dry and desert-like environments. The spines and thorns protect the plant from humans and animals. The roots are spread out far and wide in the ground for collecting water and storing it for future use. The stems are thick enough to store water. There are certain varieties of cacti that can go on for two years without water.

244 **Huntington Desert Garden in San Marino, California, USA, is the oldest of its kind and has the largest collection of cacti and succulents in the world.** Besides these, the garden also boasts of many varieties of desert plants. It is spread over 10 acres and largely displays xerophytes

(plants that adapt to extremely dry conditions), with around 5,000 species in the garden. The most spectacular cacti display includes 500 bright-yellow-spined golden barrel cactus plants; the largest among them is 85 years old.

245 **The largest cactus garden in Asia.** The National Cactus and Succulent Botanical Garden and Research Centre, known as the Cactus Garden, is spread over seven acres in Panchkula, Haryana, India. The garden was established in 1987 and is known for its rare and endangered species of cacti, succulents and other desert plants. It boasts of more than 3,500 species of cacti, many of them endangered. Dr J.S. Sarkaria, a surgeon, who also served as a captain in the Indian Medical Services, founded it. After retiring from the Indian Army, he designed and created it and also donated his personal cacti collection to the Haryana Urban Development Association. After his death in 2004, the garden was renamed Dr J.S. Sarkaria National Cactus and Succulent Botanical HUDA Garden and Research Centre.

246 **A family-run cactus garden!** The Moorten Botanical Garden and Cactarium, Palm Springs, USA, is spread over only an acre, but it contains more than 3,000 species of cacti and other desert plants. This museum of cacti is the living legacy of biologist Patricia and her husband Chester 'Cactus Slim' Moorten, who moved to Palm Springs in the 1930s. The couple worked for celebrities such as Walt Disney, helping to design his amusement park, which later became the popular and famous Disneyland. Over time, they built up their collection of desert plants at their home, Cactus Castle, which opened to the public in 1938. The gardens continue to be looked after by their son Clark.

247 **Kaktus København, Copenhagen, is an initiative of a local Danish grower, who is lovingly called the 'Cactus Man'.** It has more than 150 different species of cacti and succulents on display and for sale.

248 **The Exotic Garden of Monaco is located on a small cliff overlooking the bay of Monaco.** Besides the stunning view, the garden showcases more than 1,000 specimens of cacti, succulents and desert plants. Inaugurated in 1933, it was the initiative of the head of state Prince Albert I, when he acquired the land in 1912 and commissioned Louis Notari, the chief engineer of Monaco, to turn it into a garden.

249 **Desert City, Madrid, Spain, is the largest cactus garden in Europe.** It was transformed from an industrial wasteland into a biotechnology nursery by a local firm, Garciagerman Arquitectos. The initiative was aimed at educating the public about ecological waste and its impact on the environment. They converted 54,000 square feet into a cactus garden for its natural beauty and to show the benefits of xerophytes (plants requiring less water to survive). More than 400 species of xerophytes are on display here.

250 **Cacti are native to the Americas.** They are found from South America all way to Canada. Cacti generally thrive in dry weather, hot temperature and desert-like conditions. They can sustain itself in a place prone to drought as well. The oldest cactus fossil is found in Utah, USA, and is believed to be about 50 million years old.

251 **All types of cactus are capable of flowering.** Irrespective of the variety of the cactus, it can produce flowers, depending on the age and the climatic conditions. The age of the plant also plays an important role in blooming. Most cacti do not bear flowers until they reach maturity and some cacti produce flowers only after 30 years.

252 **Cacti are of different shapes and colours.** Cacti can be bluish, green or brownish, and can be shaped like trees; they can be round or cylindrical in shape.

253 **What do thorns do in cacti?** Most species of cacti lose their leaves as they grow older, keeping only the spines, which are actually highly modified leaves. Thorns protect the plant against herbivores, and help in preventing water loss by reducing air flow close to the cactus. In the absence of any true leaves, the main function of photosynthesis is carried out by the stem of the plant.

254 **Cactus lifespans typically range from 10 to 200 years, depending on the species.** Cacti growing outdoors in ideal conditions tend to live longer than those cultivated

as houseplants. The longest living cactus is thought to be the saguaro cactus, native to the desert of Arizona and Mexico. It is believed that this variety can live as long as 150 to 200 years.

255 **There are about 1,500 to 2,000 different species of cacti.** Each is categorized broadly under two types – 'opuntias' and 'cactoids'. They generally have round or flat shapes with fleshy interior and no leaves. The thorns, called spines, can vary in length, depending on the variety of the cactus.

256 **Certain kinds of cacti have fruit that are a popular source of food.** The dragon fruit is now widely grown in Asia. The prickly pear or Indian fig are varieties of cacti, wherein both the fruit (called *tuna* in Spanish) and the pads (called *nopal* in Spanish) can be eaten.

257 **Water stored in cactus is not clear water.** As a special trait, cacti are able to collect and store a lot of water in their stems for future use. The water is not pure or clear water and it is not suitable for drinking. In fact, it is a thick liquid, which is white in colour.

258 **Desert cacti are different.** They are the only variety that can survive in the desert. Globular cacti, with a round shape, have less surface area to lose water through evaporation. They also survive the harsh desert conditions due to their structural adaptations. These cacti continue to photosynthesize because they have fixed spines instead of leaves. The green stems produce the plant's food, but lose less water than leaves because of their sunken pores and the waxy coating on the stem's surface.

259 ***Blossfeldia liliputana* is the smallest desert cactus in the world.** This species, found in South America, is less than an inch in diameter when fully grown.

260 **Not all deserts have cacti!** It is generally believed that all deserts are populated by cacti, but in reality, cacti are only native to the Americas. The Sahara Desert in Africa only has bushes, dunes and bare rock, but the region does have plants known as euphorbias that look and act like cacti.

261 **Aloe vera is similar to a cactus in appearance, but it is not a cactus.** It belongs to a succulent category of plants and is a member of the lily family.

262 The tallest cactus in the world is *Pachycereus pringlei*, also known as the Mexican giant cardon or elephant

cactus, in Baja California, Mexico. A specimen of the cardon variety of cactus is the tallest living cactus in the world, with a maximum recorded height of 19 m with a stout trunk of up to one metre in diameter, and several straight branches. The name cardon is derived from a Spanish word *cardo*, which means thistle.

263 **Wild cacti are an endangered species.** Cacti growing in the wild are threatened by extensive animal grazing, construction and by the collectors of such species of cacti. Such cacti all over the world are now included in the Convention on International Trade in Endangered Species of Wild Fauna and Flora. Most species can only be exported if proper licensing is done and permissions are issued for their export, whereas some species of wild cacti are on the endangered species list, which means they can be exported only for scientific purposes.

264 **All cacti are succulents, but not all succulents are cacti!** In order for a succulent to be considered a cactus it must have areoles, small, round, cushion-like mounds of flesh which results in the growth of spines, hair, flowers in a cactus. Areoles are present only in cacti and not in all succulents.

265 **A moving cactus!** The *Stenocereus eruca*, known as the 'Wandering Devil', is a cactus that can move up to 60 centimetres a year! It grows horizontally, growing

at the top of the stems and dying at the bottom, and it seems like it is moving like a centipede or caterpillar! This extraordinary species of cactus is found in the northwestern Mexican state of Baja California Sur, and is the only moving cactus species in the world. This cactus grows parallel to the ground, and when it is firmly entrenched in the desert soil, the old part dies and rots, turning into nutrients that help the new stem to grow. In this way, the cactus 'crawls' or 'wanders' through the desert. Because of its unusual properties, and the subsequent demand for this rare species, this cactus is facing extinction.

8

HERBS AND SPICES

A herb is a small plant with green, dainty stems with no woody tissue. Generally, they have few or no branches. Herbs are sometimes eaten, or used as flavouring agents. Some are also used as medicines.

266 **Herbs and spices are similar but not the same.** Herbs are plant leaves (fresh or dried) while spices are every other part of the plant including roots, stems, flowers, seeds, bulbs and berries (most commonly dry). This means that plants with edible leaves and seeds are both herbs and spices, so you can have two very different flavours and products from the same plant. Fenugreek, for example, a plant widely used in Indian food, is sold in both golden seed and green herb form.

267 Parsley is very effective in getting rid of bad breath. The practice of using parsley to freshen up one's breath is not new. The fresh, strong flavour of the herb makes it an excellent natural deodorizer. The dark green colour of parsley indicates a high level of chlorophyll, which is known to have some anti-bacterial properties.

268 **Many herbs have healing properties.** Herbs such as aloe vera have health benefits. Aloe vera juice helps to soothe burns and cuts. It is also used to reduce belly fat and to get rid of stomach ailments. Calendula, known to cure skin rashes and sunburns, is used extensively in herbal skin creams.

269 **Herbs have been used in medicines for a long, long time.** Ayurveda is a branch of medicine that has its roots in the Indian subcontinent. Naturally found herbs are the key ingredients in Ayurvedic medicine. Herbs are used to cleanse the body, defend against diseases, improve and increase mind agility, and boost energy.

270 **Even in the Western world, in ancient times, herbs were used to treat ailments.** The apothecary (person who made and sold medicines by combining various herbs and plants) would mix up herbs to make a paste or a dry mixture to cure various ailments.

271 **Saffron is one of the most expensive spices in the world.** This is because the vibrant threadlike spice has to be harvested by hand. Saffron comes from the stigma of the *Crocus sativus*, and each crocus contains only 3–5 stigma. This means that one hundred flowers are needed to produce only one gram of saffron. Thankfully, only a few strands are needed to infuse a dish with intense flavour and a mild orangish hue.

272 **Saffron has been grown in Kashmir for over a hundred years.** However, Iran is the largest producer of saffron in the world with over 90 per cent of the total world production coming from there.

273 **There's a school for spices.** The Indian Institute of Spices Research in Kozhikode, Kerala, is dedicated exclusively to conducting research on ten spice crops: black pepper, cardamom, cinnamon, clove, garcinia, ginger, nutmeg, paprika, turmeric and vanilla.

274 **Two-in-one!** Dill is a plant with edible leaves and seeds, which makes it both a herb and a spice. It is used effectively in the field of medicine to treat fever and colds, cough, bronchitis, nerve pain, sleep disorders and other ailments.

275 **Allspice does not have all spices.** Contrary to popular belief, allspice is not a mixture of different kinds of spices. It is found in a berry form in parts of northern South America and the Caribbean. It is so named because of the amalgamation of aromas, which includes the smells of cinnamon, cloves and various other recognizable spices.

276 **Peppermint confuses ants!** Crushed mint leaves or dry mint powder, when sprinkled on an ant trail, tends to break their continuous movement.

277 **The most scented part of garlic is not the clove.** Contrary to popular belief, it is the white flowers of the plant that are the most aromatic.

278 **A herbal bouquet of insect repellent.** Instead of a pungent smelling insect repellent, a bouquet of hibiscus, catnip, basil, lemongrass and peppermint can be used effectively to repel insects and mosquitoes.

279 **Cloves are among the earliest spices known!** The earliest written record suggests that cloves were among the first spices used. It is believed that around 1700 BCE, cloves were used in Mesopotamia (modern-day Syria, Turkey and Iraq).

280 **The oldest known spice is believed to be cinnamon.** Merchants from Indonesia started trade in cinnamon from East Africa and Madagascar. Cinnamon comes from the bark of the cinnamon tree, which can grow up to 18 metres. Cinnamon sticks are also called quills. It is used in both sweet and salty dishes and is also a well-known ingredient in beauty products.

281 **Many herbs are said to have anti-ageing properties.** Popular herbs such as ginseng, turmeric, bilberry and *gotu kola* (centella) are a few of the most popular ingredients in anti-ageing creams, drinks and medicines.

282 **Vanilla flavouring comes from the pod of an orchid, *Vanilla planifolia*.** Though the pods are called vanilla beans, they are more closely related to corn than green beans. It is the second most expensive herb after saffron, and is popular in baking and perfume-making.

283 **Holy basil, also known as *tulsi*, is effective in treating colds and flu.** It is also known to relieve respiratory infections, asthma and seasonal allergies. It is an excellent mouth freshener and is used in chewing gums, mouth sprays, toothpastes, ice creams and cosmetics. The tallest know basil plant in world records is 11 feet high.

284 **Ancient Romans were under the impression that eating thyme or bathing in it would protect one from being poisoned.** They also burned bundles of thyme before battle in order to evoke courage in a soldier. Years later, during the time of the Black Death (plague), thyme was one of the herbs that was placed into bundles and worn around one's neck in the hope of protecting oneself

from the disease. In Victorian times, thyme became associated with fairies. Children would hide near patches of thyme in woods, hoping to catch a glimpse of the magical creatures.

285 **First found in ancient Greece, oregano was believed to have been created by the goddess Aphrodite.** In Greek, oregano is loosely translated to 'joy of the mountains'. For many years, oregano was used medicinally, mostly as an antiseptic, and to help soothe headaches, acne, canker sores and toothaches. It is now commonly used in cooking.

286 **Lavender is a versatile herb.** In cooking, it can be infused into sugar, creating a unique flavour in cakes and other baked items. It can also be mixed into tea blends and enjoyed as a hot beverage. The most common

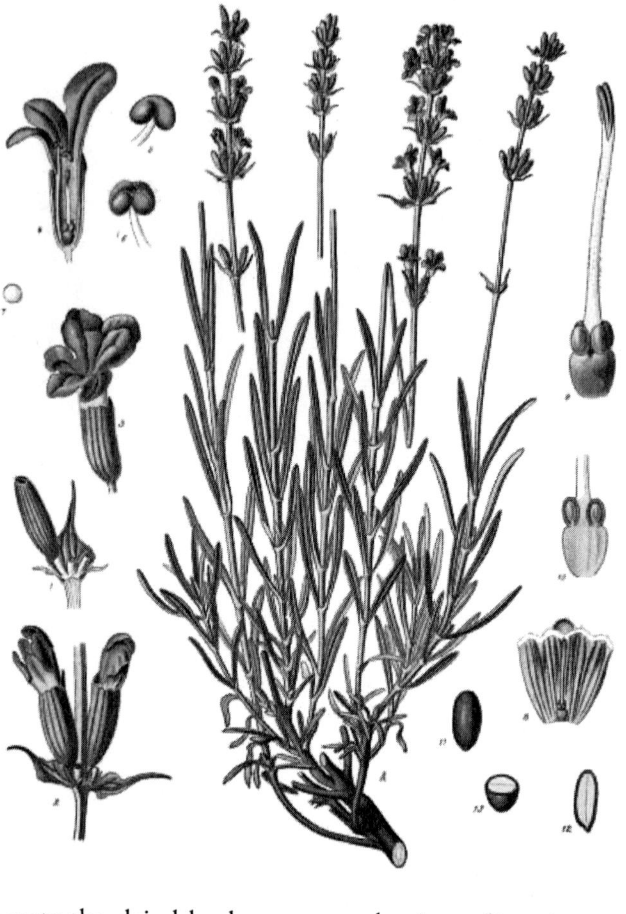

use puts the dried herb as a popular ingredient in soaps, lotions and perfumes. The use of lavender as a perfume started probably as far back as in ancient Egypt when women soaked in herbal lavender baths. Before the use of indoor plumbing when people could take regular showers, sweet-smelling lavender was worn as a corsage to mask unpleasant odours.

287 **Native to India, turmeric was also used to treat inflammation hundreds of years ago.** It was also a powerful colouring agent used for dyeing. Today the components of this spice are being researched to support its role as an antioxidant and cancer-fighting agent, and it is gaining popularity all over the world, in new avatars such as turmeric latte!

288 Like Ceylon (now Sri Lanka), the home of cinnamon, the Portuguese gained control of the Banda Islands for their nutmeg during their explorations in 1511. The Dutch and English also fought bitterly with Portugal for control of this valuable resource. There were several wars fought for control of this spice during the seventeenth century, and the unfortunate victims of the war were the native people of the isles. The country that ended up with control of the island eventually was Holland. By the nineteenth century, during one of the Napoleonic wars, the British had secretly transplanted a few nutmeg plants out of the Banda Islands, finally giving the world more access to this spice, and thus ending the Dutch stronghold on the seasoning.

289 **The names of many spice blends are shrouded in mystery.** One of these is the Argentinean blend, chimichurri. One story is that Basque colonists named the sauce *tximitxurry*, which loosely translates to 'a mix of many things, in no particular order'.

290 **One raw bell pepper has 3-4 times more vitamin C than an orange.** Paprika (made from bell or chilli peppers of varying 'heat') also contains a lot more vitamin C than any fruit in the citrus family. Like allspice, chilli peppers were also discovered by explorer and navigator Christopher Columbus.

291 Pepper was mentioned in texts related to Indian cuisines and dating back to the fourth century BCE.

292 **In ancient Egypt coriander was included as one of the foods for the departed.** It was mentioned in texts as early as 1152 BCE in Rome, Egypt, India and China. There are several mentions of it in the Bible.

293 **Originally used for its medicinal benefits, rosemary was known as the herb of memory and energy.** Bathing with rosemary was said to preserve youthful looks and scholars wore rosemary garlands on their heads to get better at studies.

294 The name of the herb 'sage' comes from the Latin word *salvare*, meaning 'to save'. When the plague spread across Europe in the mid-1300s, sage was one of the main ingredients in Four Thieves Vinegar, a herbal combination said to protect against the disease.

295 The Trinidad Moruga Scorpion chilli, the world's hottest chilli pepper, can burn its way through latex gloves!

9

BONSAI

Bonsai is the Japanese art of growing artificially dwarfed varieties of trees and shrubs in pots. The plants are created in a small container or a pot for ornamental purposes.

296 **The word 'bon-sai' is a Japanese term, which when translated, literally means 'planted in a container'.** There is another ideology that believes that bonsai is derived from the word 'banzai', a Japanese war-cry. In honour of the emperor, it literally means (may you live) 'ten thousand years'. *Ban* means 'ten thousand' and *sai* means 'years'. Bonsai trees also live for many years.

297 **Bonsai dates back many, many centuries.** Although this art form is derived from an ancient Chinese horticultural practice dating to the second century CE, it was refined by the Japanese. Travellers and Buddhist students travelling to China would return with beautifully landscaped pots of plants called '*penjing*', an old Chinese art form that displayed beautifully landscaped plants in a pot or a container accessorized with pebbles, rocks, moss and stones.

298 **The Han bonsai garden depicted an empire!** It is believed that the art of bonsai originated during the time of the Han dynasty in China, around 220 CE. One of the emperors of the dynasty had a bonsai garden replicating his empire in miniature with hills, lakes and trees.

299 **The Japanese believed that bonsai was an art form that was meditative and a harmonious way to be one with nature.** According to historians, it was Buddhist monks who were its main teachers in Japan for many years, bringing practices of art and medicine as well as bonsai to the Japanese people.

300 **Bonsai are a symbol of peace and harmony.** According to the beliefs of Feng Shui, bonsai are a symbol of peace

and longevity. It is believed that they symbolize harmony, balance of thought and all that is good in nature. Different bonsai symbolize different emotions and meanings.

301 **Making a bonsai is more than art, it is a science!** The first and the foremost step is to choose the kind of tree you want to turn into a bonsai and start by removing dead leaves and branches. After this, several techniques such as pinching buds, pruning and wiring branches can be used to achieve the desired result. The technique should be in accordance with the shape of the tree you desire because pruning branches is easy, but to grow them back can be a task. The soil mix used is extremely critical to the health and growth of the bonsai. Fertilizers used need to be carefully monitored in order to limit the growth of the tree. Generally, bonsai are kept around four feet in height.

302 **Bonsai are not genetically dwarfed plants.** They are small trees grown from regular stock. They do not need special seeds.

303 **Any tree species can be made into a bonsai.** These plants are not grown for the purpose of getting fruit, food or medicine from the plant. It is done purely for ornamental purposes. Bonsai can be created from any species of perennial woody-stemmed trees or shrubs. The plant used should be able to produce branches that can be trained to remain small with regular pruning and wiring of the plant. Once confined to the pot, and administered fertilizers in limited amounts, the plant will grow to a relatively small size.

304 **Bonsai artists usually date their trees by the number of years they have spent in training.** Usually that's defined as the number of years in the bonsai pot.

305 **A bonsai that survived the Hiroshima bombing!** A tree planted back in 1625 in Japan belongs to a collection at the National Arboretum in Washington D.C. Its history goes back to 6 August 1945, when the atomic bomb was dropped on Hiroshima. The destructive event killed around 140,000 people, but Japanese bonsai master Masaru Yamaki and his family survived largely unhurt around two miles away from the explosion, suffering only small injuries from flying glass pieces. Outside their house, this bonsai pine stood unharmed in a nursery that was walled. In 1976, Yamaki gave the tree as a gift of friendship to the USA. But the tree's past story was lost, or at least it was not known to the museum staff until 2001 when Yamaki's grandsons visited the collection and revealed its amazing history. The Yamaki pine, said to be over 390 years old, was honoured on the seventieth anniversary of the Hiroshima bombing in 2019.

306 **The fruits of a bonsai tree are edible.** A bonsai tree, depending on its size, can produce fruits which are equally small, but they are generally not eaten. Certain varieties of citrus fruits are a good choice for producing bonsai fruit.

307 **Small is beautiful.** Although there is no particular rule for the bonsai tree to be an indoor plant, due to their size and beauty they are usually kept indoors. The smaller the bonsai, the more beautiful it is considered to be.

308 **Small does not mean easy.** Bonsai plants need a lot of care, and watering is one of the most important aspects. Under-watering or overwatering the plant is one of the most common causes for a bonsai dying or not growing properly.

309 **Pot size is important!** Another thing to keep in mind is the size and depth of the pot in which it is being

planted. Bonsai do not need a deep pot. The deeper the pot, the more moisture and water the roots will retain, which tends to lead to root decay.

310 **Bonsai need sunlight too.** An average regular bonsai needs about five hours of direct or indirect sunlight every day, just like many other plants.

311 **Bonsai can live for a long, long time.** Bonsai, if cared for properly, can live for a long time. Some of the oldest bonsai in the world are more than 800 years old. Bonsai are passed down generations as family treasures.

312 ***Ficus retusa Linn* is the oldest bonsai tree in the world.** Believed to be more than 1,000 years old, the tree is showcased at the Crespi Bonsai Museum, Parabiago, Italy. Luigi Crespi, the founder of the museum, spent ten years trying to gain the ownership of the bonsai tree and he finally succeeded in 1986. The tree had earlier been shaped by Chinese masters and during its first years in

Italy it was cared for by Japanese bonsai master Shotaro Kawahara. Crespi, along with Alberto Lavazza, has been taking care of the tree since it came to the museum. The Crespi Bonsai Museum was founded in 1991 and the tree was moved there into a glass pagoda as the star attraction of the museum.

313 **One-of-a-kind living bonsai tree.** The Chabo-hiba cypresses at Cambridge, Massachusetts, USA, are believed to be 275 years old. There are seven of these plants, showcased at the Arnold Arboretum at Harvard University. These were part of a large collection of bonsai brought back in 1913 from Japan by Larz Anderson, the US Ambassador to Japan, and were donated to the Arnold Arboretum by Anderson's widow. The surviving specimens are of the Hinoki cypress, a tree variety that is now almost unknown.

314 **The Sandai Shogun no Matsu, a five-needle pine, is a national treasure of Japan.** This bonsai is believed be more than 500 years old and is named for Shogun Tokugawa Iemitsu, who is said to have had the tree when it was already about 200 years old. Since then, the bonsai has been passed down from emperor to emperor, and they are its 'caretakers' in the Imperial Collection.

315 **The Red Pine bonsai is the largest bonsai tree.** This more than 16 feet tall and over 30 feet wide red pine bonsai at the Akao Herb and Rose Garden in Atami, Japan, is believed to be 600 years old. One of the oldest bonsai in the world, it has been given support to hold up its branches. Though its size defies its definition as a bonsai,

the red pine qualifies as a bonsai tree as it is in what is technically a pot.

316 **The oldest bonsai tree in Japan.** A 1,000-year-old juniper bonsai in the Mansei-en bonsai nursery in Omiya, Japan, is owned by the Kato family. The Katos have owned the oldest garden in the village since the nineteenth century and it was opened to the public in 1925. The garden also houses a Shimpaku juniper tree, believed to be over 700 years old.

317 ***Penjing* and bonsai are two different art forms that showcase miniature plants.** The main way to know which is a *penjing* and which a bonsai is to figure out whether it is a more refined, stylistic representation of nature (often in single-tree displays) – that's a bonsai – while *penjing* is more natural and wild (usually in a landscape form).

318 Bonsai are classified according to their height:

Classification	Hand Scale	Approximate size
Imperial	Eight-handed bonsai	60–80″ (152–203 cm)
Hachi-uye	Six-handed bonsai	40–60″ (102–152 cm)
Dai or *Omono*	Four-handed bonsai	30–48″ (76–122 cm)
Chiu or *Chumono*	Two-handed bonsai	16-36″ (41–91 cm)
Katade-mochi	Two-handed bonsai	10–18″ (25–46 cm)
Kumono	One-handed bonsai	6–10″ (15-25 cm)
Chohin	One-handed bonsai	5–8″ (13-20 cm)
Mame	One-handed bonsai	2–6″ (5-15 cm)

319 **The most expensive bonsai tree yet!** A bonsai nicknamed Old Pine was sold for US $1.3 million at the International Bonsai Convention in Takamatsu, Japan. The tree is believed to be over 800 years old. Both age and beauty determine the price of a bonsai.

320 **Winters are not for bonsai.** When a bonsai is fully grown, it can bear extreme summer and winter, but while it is growing, it is vulnerable to both. Caretakers need to keep their bonsai in part-shade in the summer and guard it against frost in the winter.

321 **The largest individual bonsai collection!** An Indian couple, Ruppa and Sujay Shah from Mumbai, also popularly known as the Bonsai Couple, have been tending to their bonsai and exotic plants garden for 25 years. They have over 500 varieties of unique and rare bonsai. They started their garden, spread over four acres, under the guidance of Bonsai Master Rudy Najoan from Indonesia.

322 **Which trees make the best bonsai?** Although all kinds of trees can be made into a bonsai, there are certain varieties that are genetically predisposed towards making better and beautiful bonsai trees. Some of these are the Japanese maple tree, the ficus species, jade and baobab.

323 **Bonsai were drawn on Buddhist scrolls.** The earliest known depictions of bonsai are found on the scrolls

of Buddhist monks in Japan. From as early as 1195, these scrolls depicting potted plants have been found in Japan. It is believed that these scrolls belong to the Japanese poet-monk Saigyo.

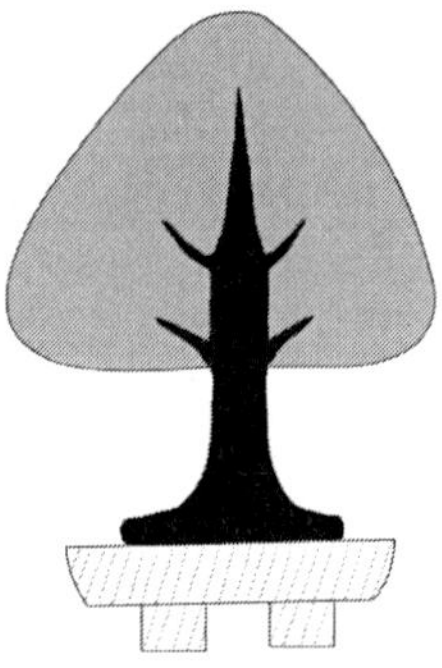

324 **Among the many styles of bonsai, there is the FORMAL UPRIGHT (*Chokkan*) style.** The tree has an upright trunk. Branching regularly from the thickest and broadest at the bottom to the finest and shortest at the top, gives it a triangular shape and symmetry. Their surface roots should be visible and radiating evenly around the trunk.

325 **There's the somewhat less upright upright bonsai.** In the INFORMAL UPRIGHT (*Moyogi*) style, the trunk and branches have visible curves, but the tip of the tree is directly above where the trunk starts in the soil.

326 **Of course, a bonsai can bend a bit more too.** In the SLANTING (*Shakan*) style, the trunk is straight, but the slant style trunk emerges from the soil at an angle, and the tip is to the left or right of the root base. In this bonsai, the branches are parallel to the ground!

327 **There are many more artistic bonsai styles.** One such is the CASCADE (*Kengai*) style, which is modelled on windswept trees on riverbanks or mountainsides. The tip of a (full) cascade style falls below the pot's base. This style is often grown in a tall, slim container, which is not otherwise common in bonsai.

328 **One that's only partly flowing!** In the SEMI-CASCADE (*Han-kengai*) style, the tip of the tree goes down to the level of the bonsai pot's lip or just below.

329 **Some bonsai are made to look like they are 'suspended' in mid-air.** The EXPOSED ROOT (*Neagari*) style represents trees that have gone through some disruptions, leaving them with bare or high roots.

330 **Gone with the wind!** Meanwhile, in the WINDSWEPT (*Fukinagashi*) style, the tree looks like it has been affected by winds blowing at it from one direction.

331 **A forest in a pot!** The FOREST (*Yose-ue*) style has many trees, usually an odd number. The trees are of the same species, but grown to different heights, like they would be in a normal forest.

10

FERNS AND MOSSES

Ferns are flowerless plants that have feathery or leafy fronds, while mosses are small flowerless green plants that lack true roots, and grow in 'carpets' or circular cushions in damp habitats.

332 **Ferns have no flowers.** They belong to the Filicophyta division of the plant kingdom. They are vascular plants that have roots, stems and a complex system of leaves.

333 **The leaves of a fern are called fronds.** A frond is a large, divided leaf. Similar to leaves of other plants, fronds usually have a stalk, or a main line, running through the middle of the frond, connecting them to the main stem.

334 **A fern has three main parts in its structure.** These are the rhizome, fronds and the reproductive structures called sporangia. A rhizome is a modified underground plant stem that sends out roots and shoots from its nodes.

335 **Ferns can reproduce in different ways.** Depending on the kind of fern, it can reproduce by spores, rhizomes or stems. One method is through spores. In this method, the plant forms clusters of spores called sporangia on the inner side of the leaves.

336 **Ferns commonly grow in four kinds of habitats.** Ferns are found growing in specific types of places: moist, shady areas; crevices in rock faces; wetlands; and tropical areas. Some fern species grow equally well in soil and on rocks, whereas other varieties thrive only in rocky habitats.

337 **Ferns are of many types.** There are about 10,560 known species of fern.

338 **Examine the root of the plant to know if it is actually a fern.** If the base of the plant is very close to the ground or soil, this indicates that the plant is actually a fern. Ferns grow from a rhizome, or underground stem, so the easiest way to determine if a plant is a fern or not is to inspect its roots closely.

339 **Ferns are believed to be older than land animals.** Ferns belong to an ancient family of plants that go back to the Mesozoic Era, about 360 million years ago. They are older than land animals and far older than the dinosaurs. In fact, ferns were the main source of nutrients for herbivore dinosaurs! Ferns have been on Earth much before flowering plants came into being. Along with mosses, ferns are one of the oldest plants ever on Earth.

340 **The lifespan of a fern depends on the species.** Some types of ferns have been known to live up to 100 years.

341 **Ferns can be grown indoors as well as outdoors.** Outdoor ferns grow best in partially shaded areas and require little attention. Those grown indoors thrive in bright light, although not in direct sunlight. Ferns flourish in humidity and moderate temperatures.

342 **The tallest fern in the world is close to extinction.** The Norfolk tree fern, or *Cyathea brownii*, named after the Scottish botanist Robert Brown (1773–1858), is native to Norfolk Island in the Pacific Ocean near Australia and New Zealand. Over time, its trunk gets smoother, showing

oval rings, which are the markings of the fronds that have fallen off. The tallest fern species in the world, it can reach a height of about 66 feet and fronds can grow up to 16 feet in length. This species is critically endangered and is protected on the island.

343 The study of ferns and other pteridophytes (all seedless vascular plants) is called pteridology.

344 **The smallest fern in the world is named after a snake!** Just one centimetre in height, Malvi's adder's-tongue fern (*Ophioglossum malviae)* is the smallest on Earth yet. *Ophioglossum* in Greek means 'snake-tongue'. Found by Indian researchers in the Ahwa forests of the Western Ghats in Gujarat's Dang district, the fingernail-sized fern belongs to the adder's-tongue variety of fern. It was discovered in 2016 during a botanical expedition. Only twelve plants of this variety were discovered, growing alongside mosses in grasslands.

345 **Some varieties of fern can be poisonous.** Owing to their small size, pronged leaves and lush green colour, ferns

are tempting to touch. But some species, such as bracken fern, are poisonous.

346 **Moss plays an important role in protecting forests.** A thick cover of moss on the jungle ground helps in retaining water and moisture. It reduces and prevents soil erosion, and during the dry season, it helps to keep the roots of trees hydrated. The moist patches of green carpet help plants and trees retain nutrients. Moss also prevents tree seeds from getting washed away and provides perfect conditions for germination.

347 **Moss can be harmful for humans and man-made structures.** Moss can be damaging to any kind of structure or roof. It may also cause problems for the people living inside it, especially for those who have breathing issues. Moss can trigger asthma attacks in people prone to allergies and sinusitis.

348 **Moss does not have tissues to transport water and nutrients!** Unlike other plants, moss does not have vascular tissue to transport water and nutrients, and so they do not have roots, stem and flowers. Moss uses structures called rhizoids (which looks like miniature roots) to attach themselves to the ground.

349 **Mosses are also known as bryophytes.** They are one of the three groups of bryophytes. They are non-vascular plants and reproduce through spores instead of seeds and flowers.

350 **There are more than 14,000 species of bryophytes around the world.** They are found in an array of colours and sizes on all seven continents. Their colours could range from green and red to bronze-mahogany and glowing blue.

351 **Moss could have been one of the triggers of the first ice age!** Scientists at the University of Exeter, UK, have reported that moss could be one of the reasons for causing the first ice age (around 2.4 to 2.1 billion years ago). So far, there have been five ice ages in the history of Earth. The growth and spread of non-vascular land plants may have drawn enough carbon dioxide from the air to accelerate the growth of ice sheets. The air then started cooling down, resulting in the freezing of water and its surroundings, ending up with the ice age.

352 **Most species of moss have leaves measuring only one cell in thickness.** A cell is only about 2–4 microns thick; therefore the thickness of the leaf is close to that.

353 **Mosses can absorb water from the air.** Moss and all varieties of bryophytes can absorb water from air unlike most plants that absorb water from the ground.

354 **Moss has healing properties.** During the Second World War (1939–45), when doctors of the Allied powers (mainly Britain, France, Russia and the USA) ran out of cotton, they used moss to clean the wounds of the wounded soldiers. Peat moss was extensively used because it is high in absorption and antiseptic properties. Millions of moss bandages were produced in Europe and America around this time.

355 **Moss can measure the amount of pollution in the air.** Since moss absorbs water from the air, it also ends up absorbing whatever is present in the air in the process, including pollutants. The level of cadmium (one of the main air pollutants) indicates the level of air pollution, or the air quality index, of an area.

356 **Moss was used in early diapers!** Ancient cultures used moss to toilet-train their children. Moss is believed to absorb liquid 20 times more than its weight and can easily be discarded, making it an ideal choice for diapers. The Chukchi people, who live in far-eastern Russia, carried their babies in fur bags with flaps filled with dry moss. When the child cried, you changed the moss!

357 **Moss can grow on anything unlike other plants and trees.** The root-like rhizoids allow moss to attach itself to any kind of surface.

358 **Moss can save the environment.** Peat bog, a variety of moss, alone can hold up to 455 giga tonnes of carbon dioxide. It is a good way to reduce pollution!

359 **Some varieties of moss help other plants grow.** Peat moss, also known as sphagnum, is commonly used by plant lovers and avid gardeners to support undernourished plants and soil.

360 **Some plants called mosses are not!** Spanish moss and Irish moss are not actually mosses. Spanish moss (a bromeliad from the pineapple and succulent plant family!) is used for insulation and furniture stuffing, whereas Irish moss (which is a red algae) is used as a thickener.

361 **The tallest moss is the *Dawsonia superba*.** Contrary to popular belief, not all moss is small. The *Dawsonia superba* grows up to 60 centimetres in height and is the tallest self-supporting moss in the world. It is mostly found in New Zealand and Australia.

362 **The yellowish-green colour of moss is generally referred to as 'moss green'.** It is found on many colour shade cards.

363 **Reindeers love moss, it is said.** But it's not really moss they eat. In winter, they depend on lichens called reindeer moss, which has a high amount of carbohydrates. They get to this by digging holes in the snow.

364 **Eco-graffiti, also known as guerrilla gardening, is done using moss.** It is a kind of art in which moss is used to decorate the walls of buildings, such as houses and offices. In this form, artists use living moss to write on the walls by blending moss and painting with it on a wall. The moss then grows in that position and forms an 'artwork' or a message.

11

DEADLY PLANTS

Plants are the lifeline of the earth, yet seemingly harmless plants can prove deadly. From the poisonous hemlock to the dangerous nightshade, here are some of the deadliest plants in the world.

365 Water hemlock is one of the most poisonous plants in the world. This plant belongs to the carrot family and it resembles celery, but eating it can be fatal. The death sentence of Greek philosopher Socrates was the result of his asking his students many probing questions on political and philosophical issues, because of which he was accused of moral corruption. At the trial, the majority of the decision-makers agreed to a sentence of death to be executed by making Socrates drink a poisonous beverage of hemlock. The result of water hemlock poisoning includes painful convulsions, abdominal cramps, nausea and

He drank the contents as though it were a draught of wine

death in some cases. If one is lucky enough to survive, the lasting effects could include amnesia and tremors.

366 **Rhubarb leaves can be very poisonous.** The leaves contain kidney-damaging and potentially fatal amounts of oxalic acid. But the plant's stalks are totally safe to eat and good for health.

367 White snakeroot is a potently poisonous plant. The plant is deadly even in the cases of secondary poisoning! For example, milk from livestock that have grazed on this plant has found to be laced with its poison. The symptoms include appetite loss, nausea, weakness, abdominal pain, and even death in some cases.

368 **The secret about castor.** Castor bean seeds are the primary source of castor oil, yet the seed contains ricin, which results in severe diarrhoea, seizures and death on some occasions.

369 There's something dangerous about the rosary pea. The seeds from this plant are used to make prayer rosaries. An unbroken seed is not dangerous at all until it is cracked

open or scratched. The chemical abrin present in the seeds can result in organ failure within a few days. It is commonly known as jequirity bean and has been traditionally used in jewellery making for weighing precious metals like gold.

370 **Oleander is generally grown as a hedge or an ornamental plant.** You look at its lovely pink flowers, and you wouldn't guess that it contains deadly glycosides that can cause cardiac arrest if consumed. In fact, people are known to have fallen sick after eating the honey made from the nectar that's made from this plant's flowers.

371 Sweet but deadly. Berries of the deadly nightshade are sweet to taste, but the fruit of the plant contains chemicals called atropine and scopolamine, which can cause paralysis when eaten. The plant's leaves are poisonous too and can cause severe skin irritation.

372 **Pitcher plants are non-vegetarian!** Tropical pitcher plants are carnivorous in nature. In order to capture its

prey, the leaves of the plant fold in what is known as the 'pitfall trap'. Once the prey is trapped in the plant's deep hollow, it produces a water liquid that drowns the prey. The most frequent victims are ants and other insects, centipedes, spiders, scorpions, and also sometimes snails and frogs!

373 **Pitcher plants are native to parts of South East Asia, India, Madagascar and Australia.** There are at least around 170 varieties of pitcher plants. The largest one can catch prey as large as a lizard and a mid-sized frog. The prey is killed in three zones of the plant – the 'attraction' zone, the 'slip' zone, and the 'digestive' zone. The plants are called 'Nepenthe', which in Greek means 'without grief'.

374 ***Aconitum napellus*** **has nice purple flowers, but it is one of the most poisonous plants in the world.** Poisoning from this plant can lead to numbness, vomiting and even death in some cases. Due to the colour of its flowers, it is also called 'Purple Poison'. In ancient times, arrowheads were daubed with its poison for hunting. In ancient Rome, it was used to execute people.

375 **Heliamphora is also known as the sun pitcher.** The plant's tube-shaped leaf becomes the organ to trap prey, such as an insect. When the prey fall into this tube filled with 'digestive liquid', they are quickly devoured with the help of bacteria in the liquid.

376 **Byblis, also called the rainbow plant, captures its prey using adhesive or glue-like**

traps. The plant's leaves are covered with small hairs, which are in fact the traps that secrete a liquid to attract insects or other prey.

377 **Utricularia, a common species of carnivorous plants, is also known as bladderwort.** This plant has the most complex trap among such plants. This is a bag-like structure, which hangs from its branches to capture its prey. Hairs and antennae attract the prey towards the trap's opening.

378 The Suicide Tree (*Cerbera odollam*) claimed the most victims in Madagascar, where it was used in 'trials by

ordeal'. Its fruit seed is very poisonous due to cerberin, which disrupts the heart's rhythm, often with fatal results. Basically, if you were accused of something, and you survived the poison of the Suicide Tree, you were innocent; if you died you were, well, not only guilty but also dead...! It is estimated that around 3,000 people a year died in these trials, and many submitted themselves to this process, believing it to be foolproof. Trial by poison was finally abolished in 1861 by King Radama II.

379 **Pinguicula, which means 'little greasy one' in Latin, is a kind of carnivorous plant commonly known as butterwort,** The leaf surface is covered in super-tiny, sticky hairs that catch small prey like gnats and fruit flies. Special glands secrete a liquid of enzymes and acids that overcome and dissolve the prey. This 'soup' is then absorbed by the plant.

380 **Aldrovanda has a snap-trap to catch prey.** The pale green plant floats on water, and that's why it is also called the waterwheel plant. The leaves of this species are like that of the venus flytrap. The trigger hairs on the leaves help the plant activate the snap-trap, and shut the trap quickly and completely.

381 **Australia is the most 'breath-taking' continent, literally and metaphorically.** Besides deadly crocodiles and poisonous spiders, Australia also has an equal number of dangerous plants. There are many historical records of plant poisoning of early explorers and settlers who were short of supplies or looking for new sources of food on the continent.

382 **The *Dendrocnide moroides* plant is also called the stinging bush, gympie or moonlighter.** It is called so because the sting from the plant results in such excruciating pain that the person prefers death to bearing the agony. The leaves of the plant are covered with small hairlike growth. When this comes in touch with human skin, the plant releases a large amount of neurotoxin, a strong chemical that causes extreme pain. Although it can treated, the effect of the pain can last a couple of years.

383 **Dare to step into the most deadly garden!** The Alnwick Garden in northern UK is a popular tourist destination. The garden features pretty flowers, uniquely shaped topiaries and shimmering fountains. Its history goes back to 1995. Jane Percy became the duchess of Northumberland and also received Alnwick Castle along with the title. The garden was part of the castle property and she wanted to make it into an amazing one. For this she hired the landscape architect, Jacques Wirtz, who had designed a portion of the Jardin des Tuileries in Paris, France, and also the French president's house.

At present, the Alnwick Garden extends over 14 acres and it has as many as 600,000 visitors every year. The duchess herself oversaw the selection of about a hundred-odd species of poisonous plants from all around the world to be planted in the Poison Garden on the premises. No one is allowed to touch, taste or smell the plants or flowers while they are being guided around it under strict supervision. The Poison Garden includes deadly plant species such as *Strychnos nux-vomica*, hemlock, *Ricinus communis*, foxglove,

Atropa belladonna (also known as deadly nightshade), brugmansia and laburnum.

Incidentally, Alnwick Castle was used as a setting for some scenes of Hogwarts Castle in two movies – *Harry Potter and the Philosopher's Stone* and *Harry Potter and the Chamber of Secrets*. It is where Harry and his classmates took flying lessons with Madame Hooch.

384 **Sprouting or green potatoes are poisonous.** The green part of the potato can be dangerous because it usually contains a large amount of a chemical called solanine. This chemical acts as a pesticide for the plant. Solanine, if eaten, can prove to be fatal for humans, although the symptoms and extent of poisoning vary from person to person.

385 **The most poisonous tree in the world.** Standing underneath a manchineel tree during rain can result in painful blisters, and the smoke from a burning manchineel tree can affect human vision. The tree is a native of Florida, USA. The 2011 *Guinness Book of World Records* had declared it the deadliest tree in the world.

386 **The most poisonous plant in the world.** According to the *Guinness Book of World Records* 2007, the castor plant is the most poisonous plant in the world due to its toxic seeds.

387 **Beauty or beast?** The beautiful poppy flowers are known to produce chemicals that cause hallucinations. The flower and seeds, when eaten, can cause vomiting and even death in some cases.

388 **Doll's eyes are deceptive!** Doll's eyes (*Actaea pachypoda*) is a species of flowering plant in the family Ranunculaceae, and is found in eastern and northern North America. It is also known as white baneberry. Although the entire plant is deadly for humans, its berries are the most toxic, often fatal, part of plant.

389 **The Cape sundew plant in South Africa has long 'killer' leaves.** These are covered with brightly coloured tentacles that secrete a sticky substance to trap insects. The leaf then curls around the prey, thus killing and 'eating' it.

390 **A pitcher plant in Borneo serves as a washroom for local tree shrews.** The plant has nectar that attracts shrews and, in their turn, the shrews poop in the 'pitcher' of the plant, thus feeding the plant.

12

ROOTS AND ROOT VEGETABLES

Plants that grow underground and are eaten by humans are called root vegetables. The term 'root vegetable' is applied to all such types of vegetables in farming and cooking. In vascular plants, the root is the plant organ that typically lies below the soil's surface. Roots can also grow on top of the surface or above water.

391 **There are different types of roots.** Plants have varying kinds of roots. The broad classification includes five types of basic root systems in plants – fibrous, creeping, tap, adventitious and tuberous.

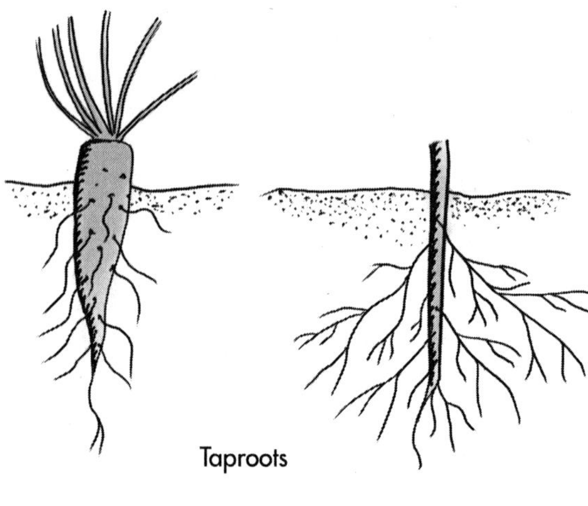

Taproots

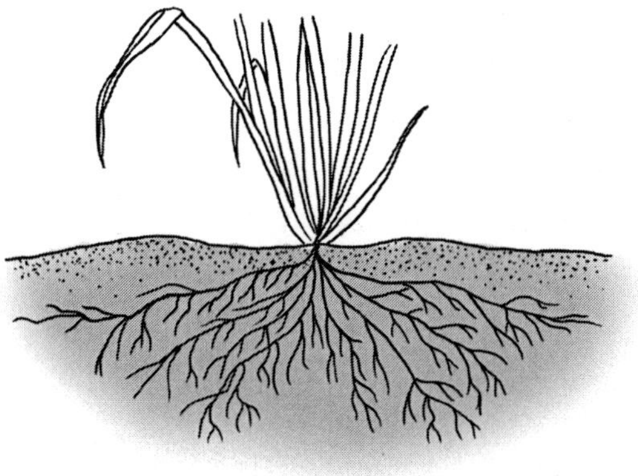

Fibrous roots

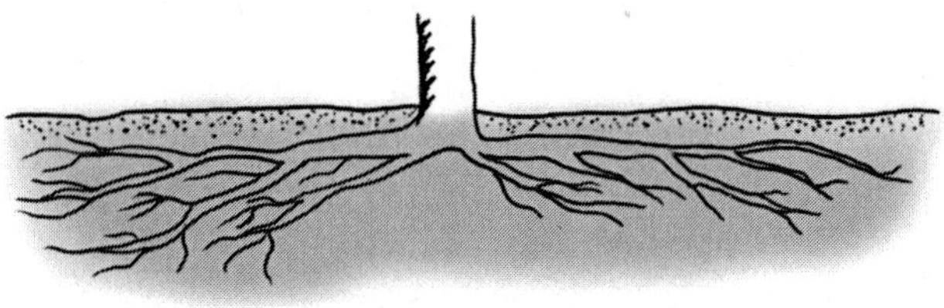

Creeping roots

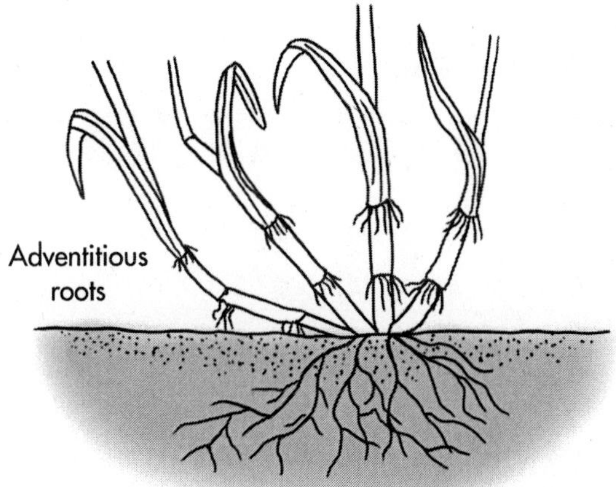

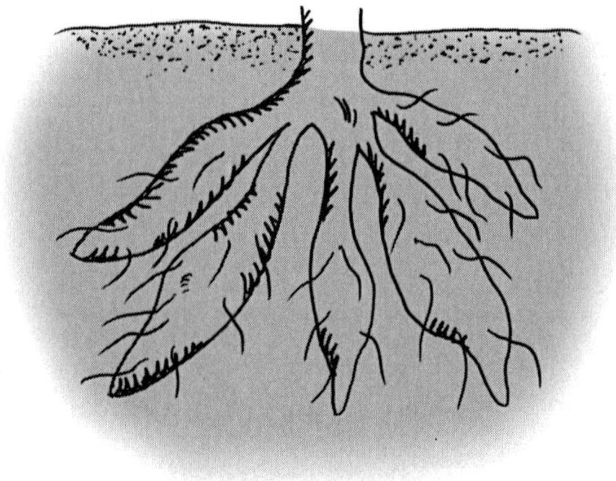

Tuberous roots

392 **Roots have an important function in a plant's growth.** They are a plant's support system. They are the plumbers of the plants – transporting water, nutrients and food to all parts of the plant. Their main work includes absorption of water and inorganic nutrients, keeping the plant attached to the ground, storing food and nutrients, and reproduction.

393 **Roots first.** A plant's root system develops before its stem or leaves. This is because roots find and absorb water to help the plant grow. As the plant grows, the shoot or the stem emerges.

394 **Root hair serves a vital role.** It forms an important surface as they are needed to absorb most of the water and nutrients from the soil. They also help in the formation of root nodules in legume plants. Root hair helps the plant's root increase the surface area under the soil, which in turn results in absorption of more water and nutrients for the plant.

395 Roots are critical for the development and growth of a plant, but some plants can survive without roots. This group includes mosses.

396 **Why do roots grow downwards whereas shoots grow upwards?** A plant's root is heavily affected by gravity, thus making it grow downwards. The shoot of a plant grows towards sunlight, hence it goes upwards. The phenomenon of a root growing downwards is called 'positive gravitropism' and a shoot's upward growth is known as 'negative gravitropism'.

397 **The taproot is a large, central and dominant root from which other roots sprout laterally.** Plants that have only one, thick, main root have taproots. The taproot goes deep and straight into the ground and smaller offshoots or roots merge into one, making a big main root. The taproot is the main root of a primary root system and grows vertically downward. Most dicotyledonous plants produce taproots, and some, such as the edible roots of carrots and beetroots, are specialized for food storage.

398 Due to their sheer size, weight and height, most palm trees have taproots.

399 **Plants with fibrous roots have thin roots.** A fibrous root system is very different from a taproot. It is usually formed by thin, moderately branching roots growing from the stem. A fibrous root system is universal in monocotyledonous (plants that have seeds with only one cotyledon are called monocotyledons or monocots) plants and ferns. When fully mature, the fibrous root

systems look like a jute mat made from roots. Some plants have small, thin roots, all of which are of same length, shape and thickness. These roots form a tuft. Some examples of plants with fibrous roots are grass, wheat, rice, marigold, maize, banana, millet, bamboo and onion.

400 **Most older and larger trees have creeping roots.** Plants with roots that are long and shallow have creeping roots. These roots do not grow deep into the soil, although they are incredibly long, so they can move far away from the plant. Due to the length of the roots, they cover a lot of underground area. Many trees have creeping roots. A creeping plant grows low to the ground, and sends down roots at intervals from its main body. Most vines have a creeping growth pattern. Other examples of plants that creep include phlox, mint, bamboo, strawberries, honeysuckle, wild ginger, plums and wild roses, to name a few.

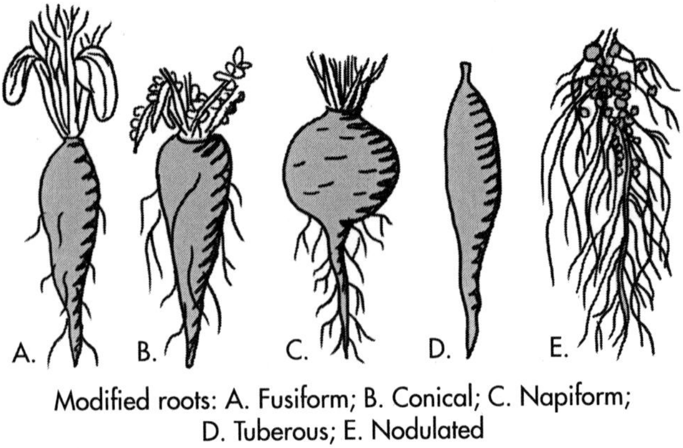

Modified roots: A. Fusiform; B. Conical; C. Napiform; D. Tuberous; E. Nodulated

401 **A tuberous root is an enlarged fleshy root modified as a storage organ with shoots produced at one end and roots produced at the other.** For example, sweet

potato is produced from a tuberous root. Botanically, tuberous roots differ from true tubers because the latter are modified stem tissue.

402 **Adventitious roots arise from an organ other than the root.** These usually begin from a stem, and sometimes a leaf. They are especially numerous on underground stems, such as rhizomes, corns and tubers, In some plants, roots start from the stem above the soil, and afterwards go down into the earth. Some examples of adventitious plants are ivy, oak and cypress.

403 **Cutting or pruning roots helps plants grow better.** While trimming or pruning a tree's leaves and branches is common, most people don't know that the same is sometimes done with roots! Root pruning can increase the rate of growth and improve the plant's general well-being and health. This practice is especially helpful with potted plants, the roots of which can become tightly wound up and bound because of lack of space. However, care needs to be taken during root pruning; if not done properly, it can kill the plant.

404 The psychological term for the fear of garlic is called alliumphobia.

405 **What is tropism?** It is the plant's movement in response to external stimuli or factors. It can be both negative as well as positive. There can be different types of tropisms, prevalent in plants, but mainly there are four – chemotropism, phototropism, geotropism and thigmotropism.

406 **Chemotropism is the growth of plants in response to chemical stimuli.** Chemotropism in plants leads to the growth of pollen tubes towards the ovules and thus helps in the fertilization of plants and in the process of reproduction.

407 **Phototropism, as the name suggests, is response to light.** The growth of a plant towards the source of light, which could be natural (sunlight) or artificial (infrared or blue light), is called phototropism.

408 **Geotropism is the growth of the plant's response to gravity.** Roots are an example of geotropism.

409 **Thigmotropism is the plant's sensitivity or response to touch.** Roots, as well as the parts of the plant above ground, depend a lot on this phenomenon. Coiling, wrapping, climbing and creeping are all examples of thigmotropism.

410 **Some plants can regrow roots.** Most herbs can grow new roots from the cutting of the parent plant. This is called cloning, which means that the new plant is the exact replica of the parent plant. Some common examples of such herbs and plants are mint, basil, rosemary, cilantro, geranium and horseradish.

411 **Root vegetables are an excellent source of nutrients.** These plants have a high amount of antioxidants and are low in calories. Antioxidants prevent or slow down damage to body cells.

412 **The root vegetable with the least starch content is celery.** Celery also has anti-inflammatory and antioxidant properties. It is said to be a magic food for many ailments such as high cholesterol and blood pressure.

413 **Root vegetables are high in starch and carbohydrates.** Eating more carbohydrates than your body needs can result in weight gain.

414 **The origin of the potato!**

The potato originated in South America and was introduced to European explorers around the mid-sixteenth century. It is the most popular root vegetable and the fourth largest food crop, following rice, wheat and maize. Potatoes also have cartoon characters named after them, such as Mr Potato Head. They also helped Matt Damon's character in the movie *Martian* survive on Mars!

415 Red onions are higher in antioxidants than white onions.

416 **Carrots are readily available in five main colours – orange, red, purple, white and yellow.** It is beta-carotene in carrots that gives it different colours to this very healthy root vegetable. Different coloured carrots have different health benefits:

- Orange carrots have high levels of beta-carotene, which is important for good vision.
- Purple carrots are packed with anthocyanins, preventing heart disease.
- Red carrots contain lycopene, which is said to lower the risk of certain types of cancers.

417 **Garlic is considered to be one of the oldest vegetables.** Garlic pods were fed to pyramid builders in Egypt to boost their stamina. 19 April is celebrated as World Garlic Day. A curious fact: Leeches are particularly attracted to garlic. They can smell it and attach themselves to the source of the smell in less than fifteen seconds, which is very fast for such slow-moving creatures!

418 **The earliest known cultivation of onions goes back about 7,000 years.** It is believed to have originated

in Central Asia or present-day West Pakistan. Libya has the highest per capita consumption of onion in the world at 30.4 kilograms a year.

419 **Ancient Egyptians worshipped onions.** They believed that the connecting rings in the vegetable were signs of longevity and eternity.

420 **Guess who produces the most onions in the world?** The annual production of onions by China stands the highest, at 20,507,759 tonnes. India takes the second spot with 13,372,100 tonnes and the USA takes the third spot with 3,320,870 tonnes annually.

421 **Also known as groundnut and ground peas, peanuts are actually legumes.** They are a great source of protein and high in amino acids. Boiled peanuts are a delicacy in some countries. For this, freshly harvested and undried peanuts are boiled for a long time in salted water.

422 **Which country is the largest exporter of peanuts in the world?** The USA is the largest exporter of peanuts with annual export touching about 200,000 to 250,000 tonnes.

423 It takes about 540 peanuts to make a 340-gram jar of peanut butter.

424 **Sweet potato is often mistaken for yam as they look alike.** They make for an excellent pre-workout food because they are rich in beta-carotene, vitamins E and C, iron, potassium and Vitamin B6. There are about 400 known varieties of sweet potato in the world!

425 **A rye plant has an extensive root system.** The total length can reach about 613 kilometres when the plant is fully grown. Rye may be a grass, but it is grown extensively as a grain and as a forage crop (to be eaten by grazing livestock). It is a member of the wheat tribe and is closely associated with barley.

426 **Parsnips can cause skin irritations.** Parsnips look like carrots but are white in colour. The leaves and shoots of the vegetable can cause burns on skin!

13

FORESTS

These areas that have trees dominating the landscape not only provide a home for birds and animals, but also provide sustenance to millions of people, besides giving out oxygen, of course!

427 **The word 'Jurassic' brings to mind the movie franchise and many, many dinosaurs.** Surprise! The word actually comes from a word of Celtic origin, which means 'forest'.

428 **At one time nearly half the Earth was covered by forests.** Now only one-fifth of the planet's forests remain.

429 **Over 50 per cent of the plant and animal species of the world live in forests.** The Amazon rainforest has the most biodiversity, which means it is home to the most number of different plant and animal species.

430 **Wood use is bad news for forests!** The sad news is that the consumption of wood across the world is estimated to rise 50 per cent by the year 2050.

431 **A green guitar forest!** In Argentina, a man planted a forest in the memory of his wife who died at the young age of 25 years in 1977. Shaped like a guitar, the forest has more than 7,000 trees sown by farmer Pedro Martin Ureta and his four children a couple of years after her death. Once earlier while flying over the Argentinean grasslands Pedro's wife Graciela had expressed the wish to plant a mammoth guitar-shaped forest on their farm. A few years later, Pedro decided to make her dream come true. The body and star-shaped sound hole of the tree-guitar are made with cypress trees, while the strings are represented by blue eucalyptus trees.

432 As much as 25 per cent (a quarter!) of all modern medicines come from tropical forest plants.

433 **A fire can help to control a forest fire!** A 'controlled burn' is a fire made deliberately in a forest to prevent a wildfire from spreading. Also called 'backburning', it means setting a fire in a controlled manner in the way of an approaching forest fire. Once everything that was there to burn is already burnt up by the controlled fire, there's nothing left for the wildfire to burn, making it die out.

434 According to statistics from the International Union for Conservation of Nature (IUCN), more than 300 million people in the world live in forests.

435 **According to the Food and Agricultural Organization, the world loses around 3.3 million hectares of forest a year, which is approximately the size of Moldova!** But several developing countries have shown that they can simultaneously maintain or expand their forests while also improving agriculture. Thus they have proved that providing food for people does not mean that forests must be cut down.

436 **Between mid-2017 and mid-2018, in the Amazon rainforest in Brazil, South America, plants and trees covering in an area around five times the size of London were cut down!** Now deforestation is happening even faster.

437 **If you feel refreshed and re-energized while walking through a pine forest, there is a good reason!** Pines and other conifers have an anti-inflammatory compound called a-Pinene, which is used in many asthma medicines.

438 **A fungus that eats plastic!** In 2011, a group of student researchers led by their biochemistry professor during Yale University's yearly Rainforest Expedition and Laboratory found a fungus named *Pestalotiopsis microspora* in the Ecuadorian Amazon forest, and, believe it or not, it can live solely on polyurethane (plastic)! This fungus is a potential solution for eco-friendly disposal of massive quantities of plastic.

439 The Sundarbans in the Ganga River delta in Bangladesh and India are the largest mangrove forests in the world.

440 **Every year on 21 March, it's the International Day of Forests.** Its theme ranges from 'Forests and Energy' to 'Forests and Sustainable Cities' and 'Forests and Education' to 'Forests and Biodiversity'.

441 **Forest Therapy is a real thing.** In countries such as Japan, doctors actually suggest forest therapy to treat anxiety and depression. It comes from the Japanese practice of *Shinrin-yoku*, which literally means 'forest bathing'. It is believed, based on studies, that forest therapy helps to reduce cortisol, which is a stress hormone.

442 **There is a rainforest inside a cave in Vietnam!** Hang Son Doong, located in the well-known Phong Nha-Ke Bang National Park in Vietnam's Quang Binh province, is not only the world's largest natural cave, but also has a verdant forest in its largest chamber. Believed to be between

two and five million years old, the cave was discovered only in 1991, and explored only in 2009.

443 **China has planned and planted the biggest man-made forest in the world.** With a view to stopping the spread of the Gobi desert, the Three-North Shelter Forest Program was started in 1978 to grow a series of forest strips collectively known as the Great Green Wall. When complete, by 2050, the forest is estimated to be be 4,500 kilometres (2,800 miles) long.

444 **Nobody knows quite why the pine trees grow in a weird 'crooked' manner in the Crooked Forest in Poland.** One belief goes that a unique technique was used to plant them outside Nowe Czarnowo, West Pomerania, in the 1930s for use in ship building. Another view is that they were trampled while still saplings by tanks during the Second World War!

445 **There is a submerged forest in Kazakhstan!** The 400-metre wide Lake Kaindy, which is 2,000 metres above sea level, was created when an earthquake hit the area in 1911. A natural dam was formed with rainwater filling a valley. Due the lake's freezing water, the underwater forest still has great pine trees that live on.

446 **Around 80 per cent of our foods came from the rainforests originally.** These include rice, vegetables such as tomatoes and potatoes, fruit such as bananas and pineapples, grains like corn, besides black pepper, coffee and chocolate.

447 **There's a whole cypress forest in a lake!** In Lake Caddo, located on the border of Texas and Louisiana states in the USA, is the world's largest cypress forest. The trees here grow half submerged in the water.

448 **The 'Forest Man' of India!** Jadav 'Molai' Payeng was born in the Mising tribe of Assam in 1963 in India and as a teenager was deeply affected by an incident when he found many snakes dead due to extreme heat on a treeless stretch of sand. That's when he first planted bamboo seedlings there, and then continued to plant and tend trees as a personal mission. Over many decades, this environmental activist and forestry worker has created a forest on a sandbar of the river Brahmaputra near Kokilamukh in Jorhat, Assam, over an area of about 1,360 acres (550 hectares). This forest, called 'Molai' after him, is now inhabited by the tiger, the Indian rhinoceros, many deer and rabbits besides several species of birds. In 2015, Payeng was awarded the Padma Shri, the fourth highest civilian award in India.

449 **Among fossils found in Gilboa, New York, USA, was also a tree known as Wattieza.** It was 8 metres (25 feet) tall and formed the first known forests around 380 million years ago. It probably did not have leaves. It had frond-like branches resembling a bottlebrush.

450 **There is a 'food' forest in Seattle, USA!** No, it does not grow pizza and pasta, but The Beacon Food Forest is still an amazing idea, which took shape in 2009 as the final design project of four students for a permaculture design course. Of the five-acre-plus project, the first phase covering 1.75 acres is complete, and the rest is underway. This forest of edible fruit, plants and herbs will be open to all and its 'food' will be available for free.

451 **The bustling city of Milan in Italy has a forest!** The pair of residential towers in the Porta Nuova district of Milan, opened in 2014, called Bosco Verticale (vertical forest), have more than 90 species of plants and trees. They are 111 metres (364 feet) and 76 metres (249 feet) respectively and together have more than 900 trees on their terraces. The designers – Boeri Studio – roped in horticulturalists and botany experts for this.

452 **Bhimashankar Wildlife Sanctuary in Maharashtra, India, glows at night during the rainy season.** This nature reserve, which is the home of the Indian giant squirrel,

lights up in this way due to the presence of a bacteria, called Mycena, which glows when there is a large amount of moisture. These bacteria inhabit all the trees, branches and leaves (even those on the forest floor) and make it seems as if the entire forest is luminescent.

453 Tropical rainforests cover less than three per cent of our planet's land area, and still they are home to more than half the Earth's land animal species.

454 **Forests cover around 30 per cent of Earth's land surface.** That's about eight per cent of the planet's total surface area. The top most forested countries by area are Russia (7.8 million square kilometres), Brazil (4.8 million square kilometres) and Canada (3.1 million square kilometres).

455 A large expanse of rainforest the size of 40 football fields is wiped out every minute across the world.

456 **The forest floors of rainforests are almost fully dark.** Only about one per cent of sunlight makes it through the thick and high tree canopy, which is a unique feature of this type of forests.

457 **The cutting down of trees in rainforests has resulted in the highest rate of extinction ever in human history.** An average of 137 rainforest plant and animal species are destroyed daily.

14

THIS AND THAT

There are so many fascinating facts about trees and plants that they did not all fit into the previous chapters! So here are a few more of them...

458 **One single mature tree can give out a day's need of oxygen for two people.** You know what an important role plants and trees play in preserving life. They not only help create an environment in which we can breathe and exist, but also help provide homes to birds and animals. They take in harmful gases such as carbon dioxide and carbon monoxide from the air, and give out oxygen. Plus, they give us food!

459 **Are there plants and trees in Greenland?** Greenland is thought to be a barren landmass with only snow and ice, but vegetation does grow there. Only five species of trees or big shrubs are native to Greenland. They are the Greenland mountain ash, downy birch, mountain alder, greyleaf willow and common juniper. The vast area has been recorded with only around 310 species of vascular plants, and most of the plants and trees grow more in the south. Greenland even has one natural forest, in the Qinngua Valley. Root vegetables, such as potatoes, turnips, beets, carrots and parsnips also grow here, along with different types of cabbages and lettuce.

460 **Can Greenland ever become green?** It would appear so! Due to global climate changes, this landmass is becoming more conducive to growing plants and trees.

461 **Ever counted pomegranate seeds?** An average pomegranate has more than 1,000 seeds!

462 **Ever heard of the Moon Trees?** In 1971, the USA's Apollo 14 mission was manned by Commander Alan Shepard, Command Module Pilot Stuart Roosa, and Lunar Module Pilot Edgar Mitchell. Roosa was a former specially trained forest firefighter (or 'smokejumper') of the US Forest Service (USFS). He had kept with him 400-500 seeds in small containers as part of a NASA/USFS programme, to compare with 'earth' seeds later. These seeds were of five types of trees: Loblolly pine, sycamore, sweetgum, redwood, and Douglas fir. They were with him when he orbited the moon in the command module 'Kitty Hawk'. Upon their return to earth, sadly the seed boxes burst while decontamination was being carried out. Later they were germinated by the Forest Service and planted in different places in the USA to honour Roosa and the Apollo mission. These trees are known as the 'Moon Trees',

463 **A plant called the northern wood sorell has two kinds of flowers!** One type of flower makes seeds, and the other one attracts bees and other insects to spread pollen.

464 **Trees make us happy.** Studies have shown that trees make people feel relaxed and reduce stress. A research

says that patients who are lucky enough to be in hospitals with 'green' views spend less time in hospital.

465 **Trees reduce noise pollution.** There seems to be no end to why trees are important for us humans. Trees absorb sound, and this could be an important lesson for people who live close to roads and highways. It is estimated that, done in the proper way, a group of trees can cut noise pollution by up to 10 decibels.

466 **Trees can reduce the greenhouse effect!** This occurs when the earth's surface gets warm due to the radiation caused by the planet's atmosphere, and carbon dioxide is a primary reason for this. Studies have shown that an adult tree can absorb approximately 22 kilograms of carbon dioxide a year.

467 Around nine million trees are cut down every year across the world to produce toilet paper.

468 **Many flowers and plants have the name of Greek gods and goddesses.** Wormwood is also known as Artemis – who was the Greek goddess of the wilderness and the hunt. The flower called Iris is christened for the goddess of the rainbow and the messenger of the Olympian gods.

469 A fully grown mature tree is about 70 per cent more efficient at reducing pollution than a tree that has been planted recently.

470 Trees that grow in city areas have a shorter life.

471 If 20 million trees are planted on earth, the planet will have 10 million tonnes less of carbon dioxide, and the trees will give out 260 million tonnes more of oxygen!

472 **There is a plant called 'Electric Daisy' that causes strange reactions in humans!** If you eat a fresh leaf of it, you feel a mild 'electric current' in your mouth. And if you happen to eat a flower, you start to feel an electric buzz (like a continuing electric shock), salivate uncontrollably, and find it difficult to talk. Your mouth turns into a cubicle abuzz with electricity. After about 10 minutes of acute discomfort, the effect starts to wear off, though very slowly.

473 **All types of tea are produced from the same plant.** The thing that makes them different is the way they are processed, treated and aged.

474 **A girl lived in a tree for two years to save it!** Julia Lorraine Hill (born 18 February 1974), popularly known as Julia 'Butterfly' Hill, is an eco-activist in the USA. She lived in a California redwood tree from 10 December 1997 to 18 December 1999, to protect it from being cut down by the Pacific Lumber Company. She named the tree 'Luna', and also wrote a book about this experience, titled *The Legacy of Luna*. The tree was 55 metres tall and around 1,500 years old.

475 **Algae and mushrooms are not plants.** They have their own category or 'kingdom' (Thallophyes) in biology classifications.

476 **Seed balls are an ancient thing.** Also known as 'earth balls', these are made of different types of seeds rolled in a ball of (usually red) clay, sometimes along with compost or humus. The ancient Egyptians used this technique in their farms after the yearly Nile floods, and a Japanese plant scientist and farmer called Masanobu Fukuoka, a leading figure in natural farming who lived on Shikoku island, revived this tradition (called *nendo dango* in Japanese) during the Second World War.

477 **Tree rings can help you know how old a tree is, but they can tell you more too!** Tree rings also help scientists and botanists find about climate changes in the past, such as a volcano eruption or other disruptive natural phenomenon.

478 **What connects chickpeas and coffee?** Believe it or not, chickpeas have been used as a replacement for coffee since the eighteenth century, and are still used in caffeine-free products.

479 **A Skeleton Flower?** No, it's not a scary one at all! It's just that its petals turn transparent when wet and then go back to being white when dry!

480 **Trees are affected by nuclear radiation too.** Not just human beings, birds and animals, but the trees in Chernobyl, Russia, were affected by the rupture of a nuclear reactor core on 28 April 1986. Not only do the trees there grow slower, but trees in the infamous Red Forest (the pine trees here all turned reddish after the disaster) did not decay even 15 to 20 years later, possibly because the usual decomposers in the environment – organisms such as microbes, fungi and some insects – were also affected by the contamination.

481 **It has been widely believed that plant matter that settles down at the bottom of waterbodies, such as swamps, can finally turn into coal through a process known as metamorphosis.** Now there is another theory that says that coal was formed from plants that had been swiftly carried and deposited due to floods.

482 Elephant grass found in Africa is called so because it grows up to 4.5 metres, as high as an elephant, or tall enough for one to hide in.

483 **Plants are like humans in some ways!** US-born scientist and plant geneticist Prof. Daniel Chamovitz believes that plants can smell, see, feel and even remember stuff... but they are probably deaf!

484 **The first trees we officially have evidence of was a leafless one resembling a fern.** Researchers have found the spread-out root fossils of 385-million-year old trees from the Devonian Period in the Catskill region of Cairo, New York, USA. These indicate the presence of wood and leaves, both features of seed plants, which appeared only some 10 million years later. One of the root systems was traced to the Eospermatopteris group of plants, which resemble palm trees, while

another belonged to the Archaeopteris group. The latter reproduced through spores, like a fern, but it is the first known plant that was large and woody, with leaves.

485 **A floating wonder!** For over a hundred years, the 30-foot long trunk of a tree has been bobbing up and down in Crater Lake, Oregon, USA. It's been doing so at least since 1896, and is estimated to be 450 years old.

No wonder that it's called 'The Old Man of the Lake'. It is said to have travelled thousands of miles in these years.

486 **Beta-carotene is the element that gives a red-orange colour to vegetables and fruits, such as carrots and apricots.** But the amazing fact is that the dandelion flower, which is not orange-coloured, has a higher amount of beta-carotene than carrot and can be eaten too!

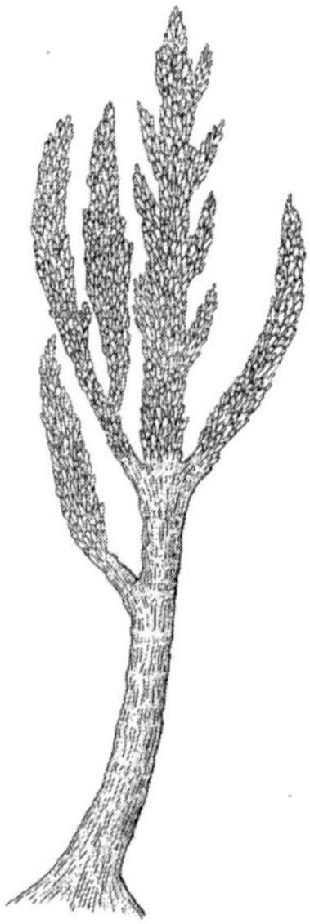

487 **Before trees appeared, our planet grew fungi that could grow as high as 9 metres (26 feet).** Called Prototaxites, these organisms had tall trunks, as much as 1 metre (3 feet) wide and were finally classified as fungi in a 2007 study.

488 **Why are red spider lilies associated with funerals in Japan?** These poisonous flowers were planted around graves to prevent animals from coming close to the graves.

489 **Olive trees are no-fuss plants!** These trees can live without being cared for! The average age is 500 years, though many live for as long as 1,500 years. They have both fire and disease retardant properties, and can also survive droughts.

490 **Artificial trees are being developed to save the environment.** With so much deforestation around the world, scientists are thinking of ways to be able to live in the future with much fewer trees. A 'synthetic tree' using resins and scientific processes, developed in

Columbia University, New York, USA, in collaboration with Global Research Technologies, absorbs carbon dioxide a thousand times better than natural trees. With an estimated lifespan of 15 years, these trees are seen as important in dealing with climate change now and in the future.

491 In the heat of direct sunlight, areas shaded by trees can be as much as 11–25°C cooler!

492 **Scientists in the rainforests of Ecuador in South America have found a plant that pretends to be ill to stop being damaged by 'mining moths', which eat its healthy leaves.** Sigrid Liede-Schumann, Ulf Soltau and Stefan Dotterl of the University of Bayreuth in Germany discovered that the plain green leaves of a plant named *Caladium steudneriifolium* were attacked by these moths rather than the variegated leaves of the same species nearby. They used white correction fluid to make many hundred other leaves of the species look variegated. After three months, they found that moths had attacked eight per cent of the healthy leaves, only 1.6 per cent of the variegated ones and 0.4 per cent of the leaves they had painted.

493 A hybrid plant that can produce both tomatoes and potatoes together is aptly called the 'Ketchup 'n' Fries' plant.

494 **A plant called *Ramonda serbica* is also called the Serbian phoenix flower, for a reason.** Even if it is completely dried up it revives when watered. It was discovered by botanist Josif Pancic in 1874 and is found in Bulgaria, Greece, Albania and Serbia.

495 Caffeine serves as a natural pesticide in a coffee plant by paralyzing or killing pests that feed upon it.

496 **Plants don't always need soil to grow!** They can grow in water, as long as it has all the nutrients they need and otherwise get from the soil. Just about every plant can be grown by hydroponics, using water as the medium to grow rather than soil. Large hydroponic farms use a web of pipes with holes for plants to grow out from.

497 **A kind of evergreen tree later named Wollemia existed on the supercontinent called Gondwana in the Jurassic period.** Once growing between 201.3 and 145 million years ago, these trees were thought to be extinct for at least 150 million years. But suddenly in 1994, a few survivors were found in what is now Australia's Wollemia National Park! That's why they are called a living fossil and

listed as critically endangered by the International Union for Conservation of Nature.

498 **The dragon's blood tree, found in Socotra, Yemen, is called so because of its red sap!** It is unusually shaped too – like an umbrella.

499 **Mosses and liverworts seem like they have leaves, but they don't.** By its scientific definition, a leaf must have more than one layer of cells, with a cuticle (waxy covering), stomata (for air exchange), xylem (tissue to transport water), phloem (tissue to transport sap) and air spaces.

500 **When a tree needs to grow new leaves, it basically cuts the old leaf off!** A layer of cells starts to grow where the leaf meets the tree's branch and these cells finally separate the leaf from the tree, making it fall.

501 **The Garden of Cosmic Speculation in Scotland only opens to visitors once a year!** This unique 30-acre garden grows on the private estate of architect Charles Jencks and his late garden-designer wife Maggie Keswick. It displays an unusual melding of physics and aesthetics, with DNA-shaped staircases, cascading and pyramidal landforms, placid ponds and many installations.

IMAGE COPYRIGHT INFORMATION

9789389253276